A Century in Books ❧

A Century in Books ∾

Princeton University Press 1905–2005

PRINCETON UNIVERSITY PRESS

PRINCETON AND OXFORD

Requests for permission to reproduce material from this work
should be sent to Permissions, Princeton University Press

Published by Princeton University Press, 41 William Street,
Princeton, New Jersey, 08540

In the United Kingdom: Princeton University Press, 3 Market Place,
Woodstock, Oxfordshire OX20 1SY

ISBN: 0-691-12292-X

Printed on acid-free paper. ∞

pup.princeton.edu

Printed in the United States of America

10   9   8   7   6   5   4   3   2   1

Contents

Chronological List of Books

Note on the illustrations: The descriptions of the one hundred books are illustrated by images from the books themselves. Where possible, the original jacket or cover front is depicted. In some instances, the illustration represents the jacket or cover of a later edition, or the title page of the original or a later edition.

Theory of Games and Economic Behavior,
  by John von Neumann and Oskar Morgenstern (1944)

The Psychology of Invention in the Mathematical Field,
  by Jacques Hadamard (1945)

How to Solve It: A New Aspect of Mathematical Method,
  by George Pólya (1945)

The Open Society and Its Enemies, by Karl R. Popper (1945)

*Atomic Energy for Military Purposes: The Official Report on
  the Development of the Atomic Bomb under the Auspices of
  the United States Government, 1940–1945,*
  by Henry De Wolf Smyth (1945)

Theory of Lie Groups, by Claude Chevalley (1946)

*From Caligari to Hitler: A Psychological History of the German
  Film,* by Siegfried Kracauer (1947)

The Coming of the French Revolution,
  by Georges Lefebvre (1947)

The Dehumanization of Art, and Notes on the Novel,
  by José Ortega y Gasset (1948)

The Idea of a Theater: A Study of Ten Plays,
  by Francis Fergusson (1949)

The American Soldier: Combat and Its Aftermath,
  by Samuel A. Stouffer et al. (1949)

The Papers of Thomas Jefferson, (1950–)

Nietzsche: Philosopher, Psychologist, Antichrist,
  by Walter Kaufmann (1950)

Ancient Near Eastern Texts Relating to the Old Testament,
  by James Bennett Pritchard (1950)

Morphogenesis: An Essay on Development,
  by John Tyler Bonner (1952)

Mimesis: The Representation of Reality in Western Literature,
  by Erich Auerbach (1953)

*The Crisis of the Early Italian Renaissance: Civic Humanism and
  Republican Liberty in an Age of Classicism and Tyranny,*
  by Hans Baron (1955)

Homological Algebra, by Henri Cartan and Samuel Eilenberg (1956)

Soviet-American Relations, 1917–1920, Volume 1: *Russia Leaves the War*, by George F. Kennan (1956)

Anatomy of Criticism: Four Essays, by Northrop Frye (1957)

Banks and Politics in America from the Revolution to the Civil War, by Bray Hammond (1957)

The King's Two Bodies: A Study in Mediaeval Political Theology, by Ernst H. Kantorowicz (1957)

The Society of Captives: A Study of a Maximum Security Prison, by Gresham M. Sykes (1958)

The Edge of Objectivity: An Essay in the History of Scientific Ideas, by Charles Coulston Gillispie (1960)

The Concept of Jacksonian Democracy: New York as a Test Case, by Lee Benson (1961)

Lord and Peasant in Russia: From the Ninth to the Nineteenth Century, by Jerome Blum (1961)

Washington: Village and Capital, 1800–1878, by Constance McLaughlin Green (1962)

The Production and Distribution of Knowledge in the United States, by Fritz Machlup (1962)

Linear Programming and Extensions, by George B. Dantzig (1963)

A Monetary History of the United States, 1867–1960, by Milton Friedman and Anna Jacobson Schwartz (1963)

Morse Theory, by J. Milnor (1963)

The Civic Culture: Political Attitudes and Democracy in Five Nations, by Gabriel A. Almond and Sidney Verba (1963)

Spectral Analysis of Economic Time Series, by C.W.J. Granger, in association with M. Hatanaka (1964)

Princeton Encyclopedia of Poetry and Poetics, edited by Alex Preminger (1965)

Adaptation and Natural Selection: A Critique of Some Current Evolutionary Thought, by George C. Williams (1966)

The Theory of Island Biogeography, by Robert H. MacArthur and Edward O. Wilson (1967)

Rome: Profile of a City, 312–1308, by Richard Krautheimer (1980)

Sounds, Feelings, Thoughts: Seventy Poems,
   by Wisława Szymborska (1981)

*After Hegemony: Cooperation and Discord in the World
   Political Economy*, by Robert O. Keohane (1984)

QED: The Strange Theory of Light and Matter,
   by Richard P. Feynman (1985)

*Leviathan and the Air-Pump: Hobbes, Boyle, and the
   Experimental Life*, by Steven Shapin and Simon Schaffer
   (1985)

*Theology and the Scientific Imagination from the Middle
   Ages to the Seventeenth Century*, by Amos Funkenstein (1986)

Ecology and Evolution of Darwin's Finches,
   by Peter R. Grant (1986)

A Guide to the Birds of Colombia,
   by Steven L. Hilty and William L. Brown (1986)

Galactic Dynamics, by James Binney and Scott Tremaine (1987)

The Collected Papers of Albert Einstein (1987–)

The Political Economy of International Relations,
   by Robert Gilpin (1987)

Painting as an Art, by Richard Wollheim (1987)

A Course in Microeconomic Theory, by David M. Kreps (1990)

*Prehistoric Textiles: The Development of Cloth in the Neolithic
   and Bronze Ages with Special Reference to the Aegean*,
   by E.J.W. Barber (1991)

*Men, Women, and Chain Saws: Gender in the Modern Horror
   Film*, by Carol J. Clover (1992)

Principles of Physical Cosmology, by P.J.E. Peebles (1993)

Making Democracy Work: Civic Traditions in Modern Italy,
   by Robert Putnam, with Robert Leonardi and
   Rafaella Nanetti (1993)

The History and Geography of Human Genes,
   by L. Luca Cavalli-Sforza, Paolo Menozzi, and Alberto Piazza
   (1994)

Introduction

One hundred years ago, in November 1905, Princeton University Press began as a printer and publisher in Princeton, New Jersey. With the name Alumni Press, it was the printer of the *Princeton Alumni Weekly*, acquiring the name Princeton University Press in 1911. It published its first book in 1912[1] and then, over the subsequent decades, gradually expanded into its current form: a privately owned and controlled nonprofit company, with strong ties to Princeton University, publishing books under the supervision of an editorial board and a board of trustees. The Press has grown alongside Princeton University, which had been transformed from a college into a university in 1896, just a few years before the founding of the Press. As its charter states, the main purpose of Princeton University Press was and continues to be "the promotion of education and scholarship, and to serve the University." Having shed its printing facilities entirely in 1993, the Press today functions solely as a publisher of books, issuing approximately 225 new titles a year. Transcending its humble beginnings one hundred years ago atop a drugstore in a small New Jersey town, the Press has acquired a justified reputation as one of the most prestigious and important scholarly publishers in the world.

In celebration of its one hundredth anniversary, the staff of the Press and I have chosen to present to our friends in the publishing and university community the small book that you hold in your hands, both as a tribute to our authors and as a commemoration of our publishing over the past century. We have chosen to focus rather closely on the books themselves, selecting one hundred of the nearly eight thousand we have published since that first one in 1912, to represent the history of our publishing program. With this approach to this important anniversary, we are underscoring the fact that, in the end, a publisher is the sum of the books it has published.

Immediately, I hasten to caution readers that the group of books celebrated here does not purport to be an exhaustive list of our

---

[1]A new edition of John Witherspoon's *Lectures on Moral Philosophy*. Witherspoon was the eighteenth-century president of Princeton University's predecessor, the College of New Jersey.

"important" or even our "best" books. Prize-winners, million-sellers, and even some household names have been left off. For better or for worse, we have chosen the books that we believe best typify what has been most lasting, most defining, and most distinctive about our publishing, and what distinguishes our cumulative list from those of other publishers.

The selection of these one hundred titles was not simple or easy. We began by asking our current staff of approximately one hundred employees for nominations. From there we solicited the opinions of Princeton faculty as well as friends and former employees of the Press. We have excluded from our selection books that did not originate at Princeton University Press (that is, reprints, copublications, abridgments, and other such derivations, though we have chosen to include exemplary translations). We have not included books published in Bollingen Series before 1967, the year we acquired it in its (past and future) entirety from Paul Mellon and his Bollingen Foundation. (We have included an essay on Bollingen later in this volume.) Even with these self-imposed constraints, the resulting list numbered many more than one hundred, and we faced the difficult job of winnowing it down, trimming what is truly our embarrassment of riches. The list you have before you is the effort of human beings and their requisite limitations. In the end, the final decisions have been my own. What you have here is a heartfelt attempt to celebrate everything that Princeton University Press has done for one hundred years through a selection of representative examples. From this list one can understand the contours, the range, and the importance of Princeton's publishing.

As I review the final list of books, a few things catch my eye. The first is the extraordinary collection of books published by the Press in the 1940s. Nearly 20 percent of our selections here are from this decade, more than any other decade—a fact all the more meaningful when you remember that at that time the Press was publishing on average only forty-five books a year. One clear reason for this concentration was the tragic effects of the buildup to World War II in Germany and the subsequent flight of so many intellectuals from German universities. The Institute for Advanced Study in Princeton, another institution to which the Press owes a great deal, hired many of the best mathematical minds in the 1930s, including Albert Einstein, and from the cross-fertilization of this group and the Princeton University mathematics department grew Princeton's extraordinarily fine math list. By gathering together some of the most important mathematicians in the world, the math list has proved to be a solid foundation for our publishing program, spreading outward to plant deep and important roots in biology and in the social sciences as well, especially economics. It was and remains singular among American university presses.

The influence of European refugees on Princeton's list is not, however, limited to the math list. Fifteen percent of the authors included here fled, by choice or by necessity, from intolerable circumstances in the thirties or forties. From film critic Siegfried Kracauer to historians Ernst Kantorowicz and Hans Baron, from literary critic Erich Auerbach to art historians Erwin Panofsky and Richard Krautheimer, Princeton University Press, and American intellectual life generally, gained immeasurably from the devastation visited upon Europe by Nazism.

One other unavoidable observation, and a particularly pleasurable one for me, is the great variety of the books represented here. It is often thought that university presses publish only specialized monographs by individual scholars. Whereas the monograph has come to dominate university press publishing, many notable exceptions pepper this list, and they are among our most successful books. We find here a reference book, two books of poetry, anthologies of collected texts, a government report, high-level textbooks, course notes turned into books, field guides, transcripts of lectures, introductory essays, and even that reviled category, the collection of essays by multiple authors. These exceptions, I believe, prove the rule: that this variety of genres has always been part of Princeton's publishing program. Original scholarly work takes many forms, as do books, and this list does an excellent job of reminding us all of the diverse forms that scholarly work takes.

In addition to our presentation of each of the one hundred books, readers will find interspersed throughout the volume a number of essays by prominent writers whom Princeton University Press has the good fortune of enjoying as friends. We have chosen them for their expertise on subjects that have been of particular importance in our publishing program over time: Michael Wood on the humanities; Sylvia Nasar on economics; Anthony Grafton on history and politics; Daniel Kevles on Einstein, a figure of special importance to Princeton; and Robert May on math and science. We are very grateful to them for their continued interest in the Press and their generous contributions in helping us to celebrate our accomplishments. Their essays, read in conjunction with the entries we have provided for the individual titles, will help readers to see how the history of Princeton University Press reflects much of the richness of intellectual life in the twentieth century, not just in America but in Europe as well.

During the nineteen years I have been director of the Press, three titles have had especial meaning for me. Robert Putnam's *Making Democracy Work* has had an even greater impact outside the academy than it had within it, more than any other professional title I have acquired in my almost forty years of involvement with the field of political science. *The History and Geography of Human Genes*, by Luca Cavalli-Sforza, Paolo Menozzi, and Alberto Piazza, is the only Princeton book to have won the R. R. Hawkins award from the American Association of American Publishers (for the best scholarly or professional book in a given year) since my arrival at the Press. And, finally, I had the privilege of bringing to its culmination a twelve-year publishing venture initiated by former Princeton editor Joanna Hitchcock in 1990, the *Barrington Atlas of the Greek and Roman World*. Compiled by more than seventy scholars under the editorship of Richard Talbert, this volume, for me, captures the scholarly commitment and unremitting quality that I believe characterize the publishing accomplished by the Press in these one hundred years.

Book publishing is a long and complicated process, which involves many talented people. After the author's unstinting labors have resulted in a manuscript, it takes teams of people—editors, designers, publicists, salespeople, marketers, warehouse staff, all working together and not necessarily in perfect harmony—to bring a book to its intended audience. A great many people made these one hundred titles and Princeton University Press a success over the century. It has been a deep personal honor for me to inherit the responsibility of carrying on the work of the Press, work that I consider a great service to society, and I believe the Press's achievements are well represented in the books you will find described here. My greatest thanks are due to the two former Princeton students who founded the Press those one hundred short years ago, Whitney Darrow (class of 1903) and his patron and partner Charles Scribner (class of 1875).

Walter H. Lippincott, Jr. (class of 1960)
Princeton, New Jersey
2004

A Century in Books ❧

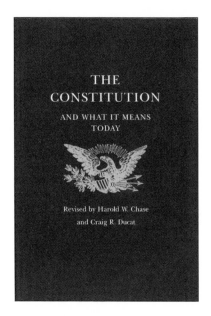

THE
CONSTITUTION

AND WHAT IT MEANS
TODAY

Revised by Harold W. Chase
and Craig R. Ducat

The Constitution and 1920
What It Means Today

Edward S. Corwin

In this classic work, historian Edward Corwin presented the text of the U.S. Constitution along with his own commentary on its articles, sections, clauses, and amendments. Corwin was a renowned authority on constitutional law and jurisprudence, and was hired at Princeton University by Woodrow Wilson in 1905.

Far from being an impersonal textbook, Corwin's edition was full of opinion. Not afraid to express his own strong views of the development of American law, Corwin offered piquant descriptions of the debates about the meaning of clauses, placing recent decisions of the court "in the familiar setting of his own views." The flavor of his style is evident in his comments on judicial review ("American democracy's way of covering its bet") and the cabinet ("an administrative anachronism" that should be replaced by a legislative council "whose daily salt does not come from the Presidential table").

Corwin periodically revised the book for nearly forty years, incorporating into each new edition his views of new Supreme Court rulings and other changes in American law. Although Corwin intended his book for the general public, his interpretations always gained the attention of legal scholars and practitioners. The prefaces he wrote to the revised editions were often controversial for the views he offered on the latest developments of constitutional law, and the book only grew in stature and recognition.

After his death in 1963, other scholars prepared subsequent editions, fourteen in all.

1922   *The Meaning of*
         Relativity

Albert Einstein

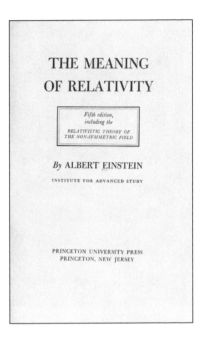

THE MEANING
OF RELATIVITY

Fifth edition,
including the
RELATIVISTIC THEORY OF
THE NON-SYMMETRIC FIELD

By ALBERT EINSTEIN

INSTITUTE FOR ADVANCED STUDY

PRINCETON UNIVERSITY PRESS
PRINCETON, NEW JERSEY

In the spring of 1921, five years after the appearance of his comprehensive paper on general relativity, and twelve years before he left Europe permanently to join the Institute for Advanced Study, Albert Einstein toured the United States to help raise funds for the establishment of a Hebrew University in Palestine. During the week of May 9, he visited Princeton University to deliver the Stafford Little Lectures for that year. These five lectures constituted an overview of his then controversial theory of general relativity, which Princeton published in book form under the title *The Meaning of Relativity*. The first two lectures, intended for the general public, were condensed into one chapter; the remaining three, more technical in nature, formed the rest of the book.

In subsequent editions, Einstein added two appendixes to supplement the lectures. The first covered advances and experimental verifications after 1921; the second discussed his latest attempts at a unified field theory (1945) and was revised for the fifth edition (published posthumously in 1956) to represent Einstein's latest comments on this topic.

Einstein's theories of relativity have had a profound effect on the development of physics throughout the past century; they sparked the ongoing pursuit of a unified physical theory that would underlie all others and explain the properties and behavior of all particles and forces in nature. In *The Meaning of Relativity* the reader has the privilege of witnessing the originator of these revolutionary theories offering an overview of his ideas to the public in his own distinctive voice.

Medieval Cities: Their Origins and the Revival of Trade

1925

Henri Pirenne

Henri Pirenne is best known for his provocative argument—known as the "Pirenne thesis" and familiar to all students of medieval Europe—that it was not the invasion of the Germanic tribes that destroyed the civilization of antiquity, but rather the closing of Mediterranean trade by Arab conquest in the seventh century. The consequent interruption of long-distance commerce accelerated the decline of the ancient cities of Europe. Pirenne first formulated his thesis in articles and then expanded on them in *Medieval Cities*. In the book Pirenne traces the growth of the medieval city from the tenth century to the twelfth, challenging conventional wisdom by attributing the origins of medieval cities to the revival of trade. In addition, Pirenne describes the clear role the middle class played in the development of the modern economic system and modern culture. The "Pirenne thesis" was fully worked out in the book *Mohammed and Charlemagne*, which appeared shortly after Pirenne's death.

Pirenne was one of the world's leading historians and arguably the most famous Belgium had produced. During World War I, while teaching at the University of Ghent, he was arrested for supporting Belgium's passive resistance and deported to Germany, where he was held from 1916 to 1918. In 1922 universities in various parts of the United States invited him to deliver lectures: out of these lectures grew *Medieval Cities*, which appeared in English translation before being published in French in 1927.

1926 The American
Revolution Considered
as a Social Movement

J. Franklin Jameson

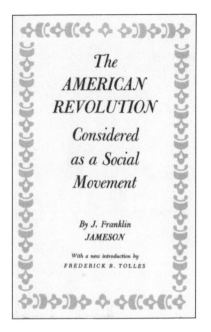

W ritten when political
and military history
dominated the discipline,
J. Franklin Jameson's *The
American Revolution Con-
sidered as a Social Move-
ment* was a pioneering
work. Based on a series of
four lectures he gave at
Princeton University in
1925, the short book ar-
gued that the most salient
feature of the American Revolution had not been the war for in-
dependence from Great Britain; it was, rather, the struggle between aristocratic values and those of the common people who
tended toward a leveling democracy. American revolutionaries
sought to change their government, not their society, but in de-
stroying monarchy and establishing republics, they in fact changed
their society profoundly. Jameson wrote, "The stream of revolution, once started, could not be confined within narrow banks,
but spread abroad upon the land."

Jameson's book was among the first to bring social analysis to
the fore of American history. Examining the effects the American
Revolution had on business, intellectual and religious life, slavery,
land ownership, and interactions between members of different
social classes, Jameson showed the extent of the social reforms
won at home during the war. By looking beyond the political and
probing the social aspects of this seminal event, Jameson forced a
reexamination of revolution as a social phenomenon and, as one
reviewer put it, injected a "liberal spirit" into the study of American history.

Still in print after nearly eighty years, the book is a classic of
American historiography.

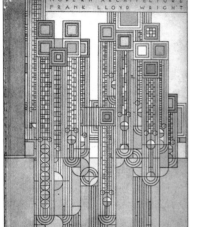

Frank Lloyd Wright

By 1930, when he gave the Kahn Lectures at Princeton University on which this book is based, Frank Lloyd Wright had been practicing architecture for more than thirty years. He had achieved fame abroad but was still little known in the United States. He was not building much at the time—the Depression had just begun, and commissions were scarce—so he focused instead on inspiring "young men in architecture."

Modern Architecture resonates with Wright's prophetic and sometimes cantankerous voice. Its six chapters correspond to the six talks he delivered to "over-lectured" Princeton undergraduates, who—according to the preface by Princeton architecture professor E. Baldwin Smith—discovered in his words "not forms but fire, not forums but ideas, not formality but vitality."

The book itself is an elegant art deco object. The ornamental endpapers feature, in salmon-colored type, fifty-one aphorisms, ranging from the thought-provoking to the inscrutable:

"An organic form grows its structure out of conditions as a plant grows out of soil . . . both unfold similarly from within."

"Good form is good sense put into some effective shape appropriate to some material."

"Chewing-gum, the rocking chair, and picturizing are all habits equally valuable to modern art."

1939   *The Classical Groups:*
        Their Invariants and
        Representations

Hermann Weyl

Hermann Weyl was among the greatest mathematicians of the twentieth century. He made fundamental contributions to most branches of mathematics, but he is best remembered as one of the major developers of group theory, a powerful formal method for analyzing abstract and physical systems in which symmetry is present. In *The Classical Groups*, his most important book, Weyl provided a detailed introduction to the development of group theory, and he did it in a way that motivated and entertained his readers. Departing from most theoretical mathematics books of the time, he introduced historical events and people as well as theorems and proofs. One learned not only about the theory of invariants but also when and where they were originated, and by whom. He once said of his writing, "My work always tried to unite the truth with the beautiful, but when I had to choose one or the other, I usually chose the beautiful."

Weyl believed in the overall unity of mathematics and that it should be integrated into other fields. He had serious interest in modern physics, especially quantum mechanics, a field to which *The Classical Groups* has proved important, as it has to quantum chemistry and other fields.

Among the five books Weyl published with Princeton, *Algebraic Theory of Numbers* inaugurated the Annals of Mathematics Studies book series, a crucial and enduring foundation of Princeton's mathematics list and the most distinguished book series in mathematics.

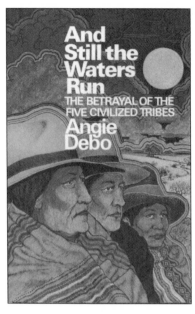

And Still the Waters Run: The Betrayal of the Five Civilized Tribes   1940

Angie Debo

Debo's classic work tells the tragic story of the spoliation of the Choctaw, Chickasaw, Cherokee, Creek, and Seminole nations at the turn of the last century in what is now the state of Oklahoma. After their earlier forced removal from traditional lands in the southeastern states—culminating in the devastating "trail of tears" march of the Cherokees—these five so-called Civilized Tribes held federal land grants in perpetuity, or "as long as the waters run, as long as the grass grows." Yet after passage of the Dawes Act in 1887, the land was purchased back from the tribes, whose members were then systematically swindled out of their private parcels.

The publication of Debo's book fundamentally changed the way historians viewed, and wrote about, American Indian history. Writers from Oliver LaFarge, who characterized it as "a work of art," to Vine Deloria, Jr., and Larry McMurtry acknowledge debts to Angie Debo. Fifty years after the book's publication, McMurtry praised Debo's work in the *New York Review of Books*: "The reader," he wrote, "is pulled along by her strength of mind and power of sympathy."

Because the book's findings implicated prominent state politicians and supporters of the University of Oklahoma, the university press there was forced to reject the book in 1937 for fear of libel suits and backlash against the university. Nonetheless, the director of the University of Oklahoma Press at the time, Joseph Brandt, invited Debo to publish her book with Princeton University Press, where he became director in 1938.

1940 The Consistency of the Axiom of Choice and of the Generalized Continuum-Hypothesis with the Axioms of Set Theory

Kurt Gödel

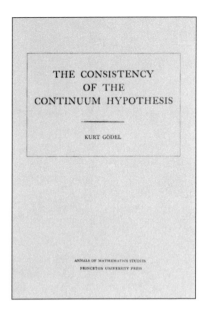

THE CONSISTENCY
OF THE
CONTINUUM HYPOTHESIS

KURT GÖDEL

ANNALS OF MATHEMATICS STUDIES
PRINCETON UNIVERSITY PRESS

Kurt Gödel, mathematician and logician, was one of the most influential thinkers of the twentieth century. Gödel fled Nazi Germany, fearing for his Jewish wife and fed up with Nazi interference in the affairs of the mathematics institute at the University of Göttingen. In 1933 he settled at the Institute for Advanced Study in Princeton, where he joined the group of world-famous mathematicians who made up its original faculty.

His 1940 book, better known by its short title, *The Consistency of the Continuum Hypothesis*, is a classic of modern mathematics. The continuum hypothesis, introduced by mathematician George Cantor in 1877, states that there is no set of numbers between the integers and real numbers. It was later included as the first of mathematician David Hilbert's twenty-three unsolved math problems, famously delivered as a manifesto to the field of mathematics at the International Congress of Mathematicians in Paris in 1900. In *The Consistency of the Continuum Hypothesis* Gödel set forth his proof for this problem.

In 1999 *Time* magazine ranked him higher than fellow scientists Edwin Hubble, Enrico Fermi, John Maynard Keynes, James Watson, Francis Crick, and Jonas Salk. He is most renowned for his proof in 1931 of the "incompleteness theorem," in which he demonstrated that there are problems that cannot be solved by any set of rules or procedures. His proof wrought fruitful havoc in mathematics, logic, and beyond.

Twelve Who Ruled

The Committee of Public Safety
during the Terror

By R. R. PALMER

PRINCETON
PRINCETON UNIVERSITY PRESS
LONDON: HUMPHREY MILFORD: OXFORD UNIVERSITY PRESS

*The Committee of
Public Safety during
the Terror*

R. R. Palmer

The years 1793 and 1794 marked the Reign of Terror of the French Revolution, a bloody period characterized by the brutal repression of those suspected of being counterrevolutionary. The so-called Committee of Public Safety, which directed the Terror, ordered 2,400 executions in July 1794 in Paris alone, and across France 30,000 people lost their lives. R. R. Palmer's *Twelve Who Ruled* is the classic study of the twelve men who made up the committee, the most famous of whom was Robespierre. Palmer approached each man as an individual, describing and explaining his inner motivations and dramatically portraying his revolutionary role. In addition, he saw the Committee of Public Safety as the prototype of modern dictatorships and the Reign of Terror as an early incarnation of the totalitarian state.

Palmer's other great classic, also from Princeton, is his *Age of the Democratic Revolution: A Political History of Europe and America, 1760–1800* in two volumes (vol. 1, *The Challenge*, 1959; vol. 2, *The Struggle*, 1964), for which Palmer received the prestigious Bancroft Prize in 1960. Palmer's key idea was that a single great democratic revolution against an entrenched aristocracy swept Western culture between 1760 and 1800, and that the American Revolution was the most important single event in precipitating this revolutionary era. These two volumes have been of singular significance for historians on both sides of the Atlantic and together with his *Twelve Who Ruled* established Palmer as one of the most important historians of his generation.

1942 Finite Dimensional Vector Spaces

Paul R. Halmos

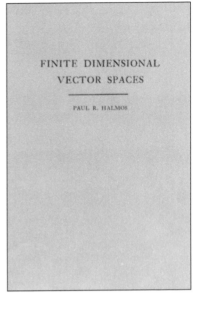

As a newly minted
Ph.D., Paul Halmos
came to the Institute for
Advanced Study in 1938
—even though he did
not have a fellowship—to
study among the many gi-
ants of mathematics who
had recently joined the
faculty. He eventually became John von Neumann's
research assistant, and it
was one of von Neumann's
inspiring lectures that spurred Halmos to write *Finite Dimensional Vector Spaces*. The book brought him instant fame as an expositor of mathematics.

Finite Dimensional Vector Spaces combines algebra and geometry to discuss the three-dimensional area where vectors can be
plotted. The book broke ground as the first formal introduction
to linear algebra, a branch of modern mathematics that studies
vectors and vector spaces. The book continues to exert its influence sixty years after publication, as linear algebra is now widely
used, not only in mathematics but also in the natural and social
sciences, for studying such subjects as weather problems, traffic
flow, electronic circuits, and population genetics.

In 1983 Halmos received the coveted Steele Prize for exposition
from the American Mathematical Society for "his many graduate texts in mathematics dealing with finite dimensional vector
spaces, measure theory, ergodic theory, and Hilbert space."

Solomon Lefschetz

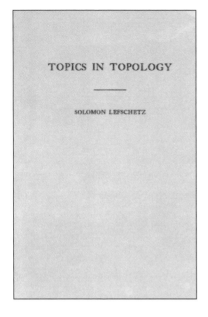

Solomon Lefschetz pioneered the field of topology—the study of the properties of many-sided figures and their ability to deform, twist, and stretch without changing their shape. According to Lefschetz, "If it's just turning the crank, it's algebra, but if it's got an idea in it, it's topology." The very word "topology" comes from the title of an earlier Lefschetz monograph published in 1930. In *Topics in Topology* Lefschetz developed a more in-depth introduction to the field, providing authoritative explanations of what would today be considered the basic tools of algebraic topology.

Lefschetz moved to the United States from France in 1905 at the age of twenty-one to find employment opportunities not available to him as a Jew in France. He worked at Westinghouse Electric Company in Pittsburgh and there suffered a horrible laboratory accident, losing both hands and forearms. He continued to work for Westinghouse, teaching mathematics, and went on to earn a Ph.D. and to pursue an academic career in mathematics. When he joined the mathematics faculty at Princeton University, he became one of its first Jewish faculty members in any discipline. He was immensely popular, and his memory continues to elicit admiring anecdotes. Editor of Princeton University Press's *Annals of Mathematics* from 1928 to 1958, Lefschetz built it into a world-class scholarly journal. He published another book, *Lectures on Differential Equations*, with Princeton in 1946.

1943 The Life and Art of Albrecht Dürer
(two volumes)

Erwin Panofsky

Erwin Panofsky was one of the most important art historians of the twentieth century. Panofsky taught for many years at Hamburg University but was forced by the Nazis to leave Germany. He joined the faculty at the Institute for Advanced Study in 1935, where he spent the remainder of his career and wrote *The Life and Art of Albrecht Dürer*. He developed an iconographic approach to art and interpreted works through an analysis of symbolism, history, and social factors.

This book, one of his most important, is a comprehensive study of painter and printmaker Albrecht Dürer (1471–1528), the greatest exponent of northern European Renaissance art. Although an important painter, Dürer was most renowned for his graphic works. Artists across Europe admired and copied his innovative and powerful prints, ranging from religious and mythological scenes to maps and exotic animals. The book covers Dürer's entire career in exacting detail. With multiple indexes and more than three hundred illustrations, it has served as an indispensable reference, remaining crucial to an understanding of the work of the great artist and printmaker. Subsequent Dürer studies have necessarily made reference to Panofsky's masterpiece.

Panofsky's work continues to be admired for the author's immense erudition, subtlety of appreciation, technical knowledge, and profound analyses.

Fragments of Modernity

Michael Wood

The whole is the false.

—*T. W. Adorno*, Minima Moralia

The humanist, Erwin Panofsky wrote in 1940, "is, fundamentally, an historian." A person glancing at the centenary list of Princeton University Press publications, or rereading certain of the listed books, might be forgiven for thinking the humanist is fundamentally a German historian. Even the very Spanish Ortega y Gasset sounds German enough in *The Dehumanization of Art*, evoking a Nietzschean "high noon" of aesthetic clarity and declaring his faith in the "unity every historical epoch presents throughout its various manifestations." But of course these remarkable historians are German only in a particular sense and represent a particular Germany, notably a Germany of exile.

The humanist is a historian for Panofsky because he or she studies "signs and structures" that "have . . . the quality of emerging from the stream of time." The phrasing is cautious and underplays the role of the scholars who fish in that stream. Emerging or nonemerging is no doubt less a quality in itself than an intricate historical process whereby qualities (of signs and structures) meet passions and interests (of cultures and persons). But Panofsky knows about this kind of argument and does not wish to engage with it at this point. It is precisely the sense of historical process that invites the idea of Germany, and Panofsky himself, in a later essay, quotes an American colleague as saying that the "native tongue" of art history is German. He is not being parochial about the matter; he insists that the discipline has also come to speak French, Dutch, and American very well. He is less sure about the English of England and notes that he has learned in June 1955 that a chair in art history has just been established at Oxford. "Hosanna in excelsis," Panofsky laconically writes. He identifies the "native tongue" as a tradition of inquiry stretching from Winckelmann to Burckhardt, Wölfflin, Warburg, and beyond, and it comes as no surprise to see Erich Auerbach appealing to a very similar legacy for the discipline of philology. "It is a German book," he says of *Mimesis*, "not only on account of its language"—it was first published in Bern in 1946. And Edward Said, in an introduction to a recent new edition, spells out the lineage: "Romance philology . . .

derived its main procedural ideas from a principally German tradition of interpretation that begins with the Homeric criticism of Friedrich August Wolf, continues through Hermann Schleiermacher's biblical criticism, includes some of the most important works of Nietzsche . . . and culminates in the . . . philosophy of Wilhelm Dilthey." The names are different but the roots in romanticism are the same, and so are the implications of intense and capacious learning. And Siegfried Kracauer, to call up another name on the centenary list, explicitly connects his own practice in writing about film to the art historian's attention to the particularities of signs and structures. "The true interpretation of documents is elicited only by the analysis of its smallest details," he wrote in a letter to Panofsky. "The 'whole' is not simply established at the beginning but is revealed at the end, as an outcome."

I can't describe much of this large tradition here, and for reasons of ignorance as much as for reasons of space. But I do want to look at a specific aspect of it in the three Princeton authors I have just mentioned. It is not an accident that Panofsky, Auerbach, and Kracauer were not living in Germany when they wrote their major works, nor is it an accident that their interest in the "whole" of a period or a place or a work was tempered by a fear of the totalizing gesture. None of them, I think, quite got to the stage of Adorno's peremptory refusal, but then Adorno wouldn't have got there either if he had not felt, belatedly, how right the apparently scattered and dilatory Walter Benjamin had been about so many things. "The whole is the false" is a modernist revision of Hegel's "The true is the whole," but it is also Adorno's way of recognizing the disorder of Benjamin's method as a more than intellectual virtue.

The content of a work of art, Panofsky says, as distinct from its subject matter, "is the basic attitude of a nation, a period, a class, a religious or philosophical persuasion—all this unconsciously qualified by one personality, and condensed into one work." The emphasis on what Panofsky also calls "involuntary revelation" is telling. Presumably the artist has conscious intentions but is not in pursuit of "the basic attitude" of anything. Certainly the notion of a basic attitude is strongly simplifying and potentially reductive. Kracauer, for example, simplifies wildly in *From Caligari to Hitler*. Again and again he sees German films as showing a country, indeed a "German collective soul," "wavering between tyranny and chaos," "wavering between . . . anarchy and authority." I'm sure the soul was wavering, but not always between the same two abstractions, and I'm pretty sure the soul was not all there was. But even as he is generalizing, Kracauer is also inviting us to look at something else in a film: "casual configurations of human bodies and inanimate objects, and an endless succession of unobtrusive phenomena." "As a matter of fact," he adds, "the screen shows itself particularly concerned with the unobtrusive, the normally neglected." In an early essay Kracauer wrote that "the position that an epoch occupies in the historical process can be determined more strikingly from an analysis of its inconspicuous surface-level expressions than from that epoch's judgments about itself." Agreeing with Kracauer about their shared interest in such details, Panofsky wrote in a letter, "It derives from the fact that we have both learned something from the movies." "Films are able," Kracauer writes in a grand phrase, "to scan the whole visible world." But then the whole includes, precisely, the "casual configurations" and "unobtrusive phenomena" that resist simplification. Well, more than resist it; they make it ultimately impossible. In his later *Theory of Film*, Kracauer evokes a series of images from the movies of Fellini, De Sica, and Rossellini, and suggests not so much that they defy interpretation as that we should refuse the interpretative temptation the images seem so poignantly to present:

> Any attempt at an allegorical interpretation would drain these ideograms of their substance. They are propositions rather than rebuses. Snatched from transient life, they not only challenge the spectator to penetrate their secret but, perhaps even more insistently, request him to preserve them as the irreplaceable images they are.

This vision of a whole that contains the means of its own undoing receives its clearest, but still rather elusive, formulation toward the end of Auerbach's *Mimesis*, which Kracauer cites on this very subject. There are "certain modern philologists," Auerbach writes, "who hold that the interpretation of a few passages from *Hamlet*, *Phèdre*, or *Faust* can be made to yield more, and more decisive information about Shakespeare, Racine, or Goethe and their times than would a systematic and chronological treatment of their lives and works." What's more, Auerbach himself is such a philologist, and "the present book may be cited as an illustration." We see from the words "decisive information" and "their times" that this proposition is not a refusal of Panofsky's idea of content, only a refinement in the method of displaying it. If there were no whole, the scattered parts couldn't be got to imply it. But in practice, divining whole works and cultures from particular passages is quite different from assertions about souls and nations, because the detail is always in the foreground. There is something shaky about Auerbach's argument that factionalism leads to fascism—an old European unity breaks into pieces and the pieces are enemies of each other.

> The temptation to entrust oneself to a sect which solved all problems with a single formula, whose power of suggestion imposed solidarity, and which ostracized everything which would not fit in and submit—this temptation was so great that, with many people, fascism hardly had to employ force when the time came for it to spread through the countries of old European culture, absorbing the smaller sects.

But what's shaky is the idea of the old unity, along with the ambiguity of the fragmentation. The diagnosis of the lure of the simple formula is impeccable. Auerbach, a Jewish exile from the Nazi regime, is writing his book in Istanbul during World War II, and as Said suggests, he is trying "to rescue sense and meanings from the fragments of modernity." Those fragments include both the parts that allow us to see the whole, and the parts that imagine they are the whole, and there is a genuine pathos in the sight of Auerbach's closely working through this dilemma, sentence by sentence. The writings of Proust and Woolf and others, Auerbach says, represent "a transfer of confidence" from the whole to the parts, and ultimately to the parts in their own right: "nothing less than the wealth of reality and depth of life in every moment to which we surrender ourselves without prejudice." But Auerbach is in the best sense too German—too devoted to a holistic tradition of scholarship—to let himself go all the way to this radical atomism; he defines the literary confidence of modern writers as, certainly, an underplaying of "the great exterior turning points and blows of fate" but not a refusal of totality, properly understood.

> There is a confidence that in any random fragment plucked from the course of life at any time the totality of its fate is contained and can be portrayed. There is a greater confidence in syntheses gained through full exploration of an everyday occurrence than in a chronologically well-ordered total treatment which . . . emphasizes the great turning points of destiny.

This passage is heroic even in its inconsistencies. Everyday occurrences can't defeat fate, but they can defeat the idea that fate is a totality.

Panofsky of course is not opposed to a "chronologically well-ordered total treatment"—neither is Auerbach, except in his polemical moments—and his *Life and Art of Albrecht Dürer* is one of the most distinguished examples there is of such a thing. But Panofsky also believes that we arrive at the whole through the parts, and only through the parts—the whole is not something given in advance. When we read his masterly pages on Dürer's *Melancholia*, we are constantly picking up distinctions rather than simplifications. "It is not so much a dark as a darkened face, made all the more impressive by its contrast with the startling white of the eyes." The figure has a "fixed stare" that suggests "intent though fruitless searching." "She is inactive not because she is too lazy to work but because work has become meaningless to her; her energy is paralyzed not by sleep but by thought." In the following quotation, the close of Panofsky's chapter on this great engraving, we can see the poise and sanity of a great German tradition, the generous subsumption of whatever can be known into a historical unity.

> Thus Dürer's most perplexing engraving is, at the same time, the objective statement of a general philosophy and the subjective confession of an individual man. It fuses, and transforms, two great representational and literary traditions, that of Melancholy as one of the four humors and that of Geometry as one of the Seven Liberal Arts. It typifies the artist of the Renaissance who respects practical skill, but longs all the more fervently for mathematical theory—who feels "inspired" by celestial influences and eternal ideas, but suffers all the more deeply from his human frailty and intellectual finiteness. . . . But in doing all this it is in a sense a spiritual self-portrait of Albrecht Dürer.

But it may be that we can also see something else in this paragraph: the tensions within the very unity being invoked, and the half-buried thought that unity may be the humanist's name for contradiction, a brave hope in good times and a desperate fiction in bad ones. Auerbach wrote that "*Mimesis* is quite consciously a book that a particular person, in a particular situation, wrote at the beginning of the 1940s." We might say the same for Panofsky's *Dürer* and, with a change of date to accommodate a larger time frame, for Kracauer's *From Caligari to Hitler*. And if we said this, we would be stressing, beyond the often forgotten commonplace that all books are written by particular persons in particular situations at particular times, the fact that these men all left Germany (Kracauer in 1933, Panofsky in 1934, and Auerbach in 1935) and yet continued to represent, with enormous distinction, a long German tradition rapidly becoming extinct in Germany itself. The humanist, in such a context, is not only a historian but a piece of history, and one of the means by which we survive it.

Michael Wood is the Charles Barnwell Straut Professor of English and Professor of Comparative Literature at Princeton University. His works include books on Stendhal, Garcia Marquez, Nabokov, and Kafka. He is a widely published essayist with articles on film and literature in Harper's, London Review of Books, New York Review of Books, New York Times Book Review, New Republic, *and elsewhere. Michael Wood was on the Princeton University Press editorial board from January 1997 to December 2001.*

Edited by Edward
Mead Earle, with
the collaboration
of Gordon A. Craig
and Felix Gilbert

This remarkable collection of essays by twenty authors provided a history of military strategy from Machiavelli to the present age. Published in the middle of World War II, the volume analyzed and described the ideas of the major military thinkers and strategists, ranging from engineers such as Vauban to soldiers such as Frederick the Great; from the statesmen Alexander Hamilton, Lloyd George, and Winston Churchill to the revolutionaries Karl Marx and Friedrich Engels.

The book grew out of a seminar conducted annually, beginning in 1934, by Edward Mead Earle at the Institute for Advanced Study. At a time when social scientists and historians devoted little attention to the study of military strategy and the art of warfare, this seminar provoked fresh perspectives on how leading minds at different times had understood the reasons for war, how wars should be conducted, and the way politics and war interacted.

Historian Peter Paret replaced Earle as the primary editor for a second edition, which was assembled during the Cold War and bore the new subtitle *Military Thought from Machiavelli to the Nuclear Age*. Paret reconceived the volume, replacing all but one essay, to confront the challenge that nuclear weapons posed, given pronouncements that such weapons had rendered war "unthinkable."

1944 *Introduction to Mathematical Logic*

Alonzo Church

L ogic is sometimes called the foundation of mathematics: the logician studies the kinds of reasoning used in the individual steps of a proof. Alonzo Church was a pioneer in the field of mathematical logic, whose contributions to number theory and the theories of algorithms and computability laid the theoretical foundations of computer science. His first Princeton book, *The Calculi of Lambda-Conversion* (1941), established an invaluable tool that computer scientists still use today.

Even beyond the accomplishment of that book, however, his second Princeton book, *Introduction to Mathematical Logic*, defined its subject for a generation. Originally published in Princeton's Annals of Mathematics Studies series, this book was revised in 1956 and reprinted a third time, in 1996, in the Princeton Landmarks in Mathematics series. Although new results in mathematical logic have been developed and other textbooks have been published, it remains, sixty years later, a basic source for understanding formal logic.

Church was one of the principal founders of the Association for Symbolic Logic; he founded the *Journal of Symbolic Logic* in 1936 and remained an editor until 1979. At his death in 1995, Church was still regarded as the greatest mathematical logician in the world.

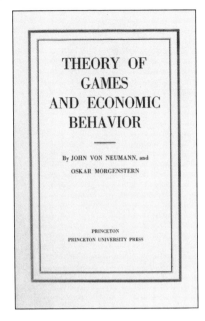

Theory of Games and Economic Behavior   *1944*

John von Neumann and Oskar Morgenstern

This classic work began as a modest proposal for a mathematician and an economist to write a short paper together. In 1944 that paper grew into one of the most important theoretical tracts of the postwar academy, when Princeton published the book-length version. John von Neumann and Oskar Morgenstern conceived a groundbreaking mathematical theory of economic and social organization, based on games of strategy. Their collaboration revolutionized economics, and, well beyond that, it yielded an entirely new field of scientific inquiry—game theory—that has been used to analyze a host of real-world phenomena from arms races to presidential candidates, from vaccination policy to salary negotiations in major league baseball. Game theory is a branch of mathematics that analyzes interactions with formalized incentive structures, allowing the study of predicted and actual behavior as well as of optimal strategies. It has become centrally important to scientific and social scientific inquiry.

The book sold only two hundred copies in its first year, but, after a front-page article in the *New York Times* the following year and lavish attention in the *American Economic Review*, it became a hit. Over time, the book has spawned articles in a surprising range of publications, from academic journals to popular magazines such as *Scientific American*, *Fortune*, and even the racing sheets.

Theory of Games and Economic Behavior enjoys a robust longevity. A sixtieth anniversary edition was published in 2004.

1945 The Psychology of Invention in the Mathematical Field

Jacques Hadamard

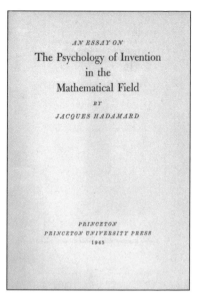

AN ESSAY ON
The Psychology of Invention
in the
Mathematical Field
BY
JACQUES HADAMARD

PRINCETON
PRINCETON UNIVERSITY PRESS
1945

When the eminent French mathematician Jacques Hadamard set out to explore how mathematicians invent new ideas, he considered the creative experiences of some of the greatest thinkers of his generation, such as George Pólya, Claude Lévi-Strauss, and Albert Einstein. It appeared that inspiration could strike anytime, particularly after an individual had worked hard on a problem for days and then turned attention to another activity. In exploring this phenomenon, Hadamard produced one of the most famous and cogent cases for the existence of unconscious mental processes not only in mathematical invention but also in other forms of creativity. Written before the explosion of research in computers and cognitive science, *The Psychology of Invention* remains an important tool for exploring the increasingly complex problem of mental life. The Press retitled the book *The Mathematician's Mind* in 1996.

Hadamard was himself a great mathematical innovator. He proved the prime number theorem in 1896 and continued for decades to make major contributions to geometry, dynamics, and many other areas of mathematics. Yet his life encompassed much more than his mathematical work. Hadamard, himself Jewish, was very active in the Dreyfus affair in France, fighting tirelessly in defense of Dreyfus's innocence. He fled Nazi-occupied France for the United States and later England, returning to France after the war. Having lost two of his three sons in World War I, and then the third in World War II, he became active in leftist peace movements.

How to Solve It: 1945
A New Aspect of
Mathematical
Method

George Pólya

In this best-selling classic, George Pólya revealed how the mathematical method of demonstrating a proof or finding an unknown can be of help in attacking any problem that can be "reasoned" out—from building a bridge to winning a game of anagrams. Generations of readers have relished Pólya's deft instructions on stripping away irrelevancies and going straight to the heart of a problem. *How to Solve It* popularized heuristics, the art and science of discovery and invention. It has been in print continuously since 1945 and has been translated into twenty-three different languages.

Pólya was one of the most influential mathematicians of the twentieth century. He made important contributions to a great variety of mathematical research: from complex analysis to mathematical physics, number theory, probability, geometry, astronomy, and combinatorics. He was also an extraordinary teacher—he taught until he was ninety—and maintained a strong interest in pedagogical matters throughout his long career. In addition to *How to Solve It*, he published a two-volume work on the topic of problem solving, *Mathematics of Plausible Reasoning*, also with Princeton.

Pólya is one of the most frequently quoted mathematicians, and the following statements from *How to Solve It* make clear why: "My method to overcome a difficulty is to go around it." "Geometry is the science of correct reasoning on incorrect figures." "In order to solve this differential equation you look at it till a solution occurs to you."

1945　The Open Society
and Its Enemies
(two volumes)

Karl R. Popper

By KARL R. POPPER

The Open Society
and Its Enemies
1 Plato

*T*he Open Society and
Its Enemies was one of
the monumental achieve-
ments of political and
social philosophy in the
twentieth century. Not
merely a brilliant analy-
sis of Plato, Hegel, and
Marx, it also served as
an intellectual manifesto
defending freedom and democracy against totalitarianism.

Popper was born in 1902 to a Viennese family of Jewish origin.
He taught in Austria until 1937, when he emigrated to New
Zealand in anticipation of the Nazi annexation of Austria the following year, and he settled in England in 1949. Before the annexation, Popper had written mainly about the philosophy of science,
but from 1938 until the end of the Second World War he focused
his energies on political philosophy, seeking to diagnose the intellectual origins of German and Soviet totalitarianism. *The Open
Society and Its Enemies* was the result.

In the book, Popper condemned Plato, Marx, and Hegel as
"holists" and "historicists"—a holist, according to Popper, believes that individuals are formed entirely by their social groups;
historicists believe that social groups evolve according to internal
principles that it is the intellectual's task to uncover. Popper, by
contrast, held that social affairs are unpredictable, and argued ve-
hemently against social engineering. He also sought to shift the
focus of political philosophy away from questions about who
ought to rule toward questions about how to minimize the damage done by the powerful.

The book was an immediate sensation, and—though it has
long been criticized for its portrayals of Plato, Marx, and Hegel—
it has remained a landmark on the left and right alike for its defense of freedom and the spirit of critical inquiry.

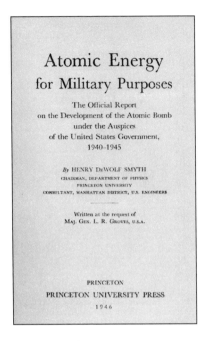

Atomic Energy

for Military Purposes

The Official Report
on the Development of the Atomic Bomb
under the Auspices
of the United States Government,
1940–1945

By HENRY DeWOLF SMYTH
CHAIRMAN, DEPARTMENT OF PHYSICS
PRINCETON UNIVERSITY
CONSULTANT, MANHATTAN DISTRICT, U.S. ENGINEERS

Written at the request of
MAJ. GEN. L. R. GROVES, U.S.A.

PRINCETON
PRINCETON UNIVERSITY PRESS
1946

*Military Purposes:
The Official Report
on the Development
of the Atomic Bomb
under the Auspices
of the United States
Government,
1940–1945*

Henry De Wolf Smyth

O n the eve of the dramatic climax of the Manhattan Project—the secret American program to create a nuclear weapon during World War II—the project's managers asked Henry De Wolf Smyth, Princeton physicist and a key staff member of the project, to draft a report about its activities. Smyth completed the report in the summer of 1945, and, after some debate within the government, President Truman ordered its public release, in a censored version. On August 11, 1945, five days after the Allies dropped the first nuclear bomb on Japan, the report was made public.

Datus Smith, then director of the Press, approached Smyth about publishing the report as a book, and Smyth accepted the offer. The book was many things at once: a primer on nuclear physics and the history of radioactivity; a chronicle of the efforts to break down the atom by bombardment; a summation of the organization of the high-powered research team; and an account of how the project achieved its goal of producing a nuclear weapon in just three years.

Despite wartime shortages of paper and staff, the Press published the book within three weeks of receipt of the manuscript, and it quickly became a best-seller. Public interest in the report was so great—with articles and reviews appearing in such periodicals as the *New York Times*, the *Nation*, the *New Republic*, and the *New Yorker*—that the first printing of sixty thousand copies sold out on the day of publication.

Claude Chevalley

French mathematician Claude Chevalley had a major influence on the development of several areas of mathematics, but his most important contribution is his work on group theory. In *Theory of Lie Groups*, Chevalley further developed the ideas that Hermann Weyl presented in *The Classical Groups* (see p. 6) by formalizing the interrelation of algebra and geometry. Lie groups are important in mathematical analysis, physics, and geometry because they describe the symmetry of analytical structures. The work was initially planned as a two-volume set, but the author never completed the second volume, though he published on the topic in a series of journal papers.

Theory of Lie Groups was originally published in the Princeton Mathematical Series in 1946; it was republished in the Princeton Landmarks in Mathematics series in 1999. Owing to the ongoing importance of Lie groups in mathematics and theoretical physics, the book, currently in its sixteenth printing, remains important for researchers in both fields.

From Caligari to Hitler: A Psychological History of the German Film

Siegfried Kracauer

In *From Caligari to Hitler*, Siegfried Kracauer—the German-born writer and film critic who shared many ideas and interests with his friend Walter Benjamin—made a startling (and still controversial) claim: films as a popular art provide insight into the unconscious motivations and fantasies of a nation. In films of the 1920s such as *The Cabinet of Dr. Caligari*, *M*, *Metropolis*, and *The Blue Angel*, he traced recurring visual and narrative tropes that expressed, he argued, a fear of chaos and a desire for order, even at the price of authoritarian rule. The book has become an undisputed classic of film historiography, laying the foundations for the serious study of film.

Kracauer was an important film critic in Weimar Germany. A Jew, he escaped the rise of Nazism, fleeing to Paris in 1933. Later, in anguish after Benjamin's suicide, he made his way to New York, where he remained until his death in 1966. He wrote *From Caligari to Hitler* while working as a "special assistant" to the curator of the Museum of Modern Art's film division. He was also on the editorial board of Bollingen Series. Despite many critiques of its attempt to link movies to historical outcomes, *From Caligari to Hitler* remains Kracauer's best-known and most influential book, and a seminal work in the study of film. Princeton published a revised edition of his *Theory of Film: The Redemption of Physical Reality* in 1997.

1947 The Coming of the French Revolution

Georges Lefebvre

Translated from the French

The Coming of the
FRENCH
REVOLUTION

By GEORGES LEFEBVRE
TRANSLATED BY
R. R. PALMER

1789

PRINCETON UNIVERSITY PRESS
PRINCETON, NEW JERSEY

In 1939, in observation of the 150th anniversary of the French Revolution, and on the eve of the Second World War, the great French historian Georges Lefebvre published this classic study of the beginnings of the French Revolution, from the summer of 1788 to October 1789. Lefebvre's signature contribution was writing history "from below"—a Marxist approach—and his particular specialty was the French Revolution as viewed from the experiences of the peasantry. Placing the "common people" at the center of his analysis, Lefebvre emphasized the class struggles within France and the significant role they played in the coming of the Revolution. With the beginning of World War II and the rise of the Vichy government in France, however, Lefebvre's book was suppressed and burned as a piece of blasphemous and revolutionary literature.

R. R. Palmer, himself a distinguished historian of the French Revolution (see p. 9), translated the book into English, earning it widespread readership and recognition in the Anglo-American world. Although recent historians have reinterpreted the Revolution and disputed Lefebvre's conclusions, *The Coming of the French Revolution* remains essential reading for anyone interested in the origins of this great turning point in the formation of the modern world. More important, as Palmer pointed out, studying the origins of the French Revolution broadens contemporary understanding of democracy, dictatorship, and revolution.

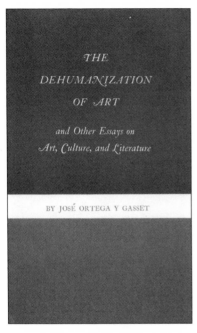

The Dehumanization   *1948*
of Art, and Notes on
the Novel

José Ortega y Gasset

Translated from the Spanish

No work of Spanish philosopher and essayist José Ortega y Gasset has been more frequently cited, admired, or criticized than his defense of modernism, "The Dehumanization of Art." In the essay, originally published in Spanish in 1925, Ortega grappled philosophically with the newness of nonrepresentational art and sought to make it more understandable to a public confused by it. Many embraced the essay as a manifesto extolling the virtues of vanguard artists and promoting their efforts to abandon the realism and the romanticism of the nineteenth century.

The "dehumanization" of the title, which was meant descriptively rather than pejoratively, referred most literally to the absence of human forms in nonrepresentational art, but also to its insistent unpopularity, its indifference to the past, and its iconoclasm. Ortega championed what he saw as a new cultural politics with the goal of a total transformation of society.

Ortega was an immensely gifted writer in the best belletristic tradition. His work has been compared to an iceberg because it hides the critical mass of its erudition beneath the surface, and because it is deceptive, appearing to be more spontaneous and informal than it really is.

Princeton published the first English translation of the essay paired with another entitled "Notes on the Novel." Three essays were later added to make an expanded edition, published in 1968, under the title *The Dehumanization of Art and Other Essays on Art, Culture, and Literature.*

1949 *The Idea of a Theater:*
A Study of Ten Plays

Francis Fergusson

Former U.S. poet lau-
reate Robert Pinsky
has called Francis Fergusson "one of the few truly
great American critics of
the [twentieth] century." A
renowned classical scholar,
translator, and critic, Fergusson had the rare crit-
ical gift of being able to
combine a sense of the
past with penetrating con-
temporary insight. In the 1920s Fergusson had theatrical training
and worked as an assistant to Richard Boleslavsky, the Russian
actor and teacher who introduced Americans to the Stanis-
lavskian method of acting. Fergusson began his teaching career at
Bennington College—where Martha Graham was his colleague.

All these experiences influenced his enduring study *The Idea of
a Theater*, in which Fergusson developed an original approach to
the phenomenon of theater. He looked closely at just ten plays—
from Sophocles' *Oedipus Rex* to T. S. Eliot's then-contemporary
Murder in the Cathedral (1938)—in order to develop a historical
continuum that captured the changing perspective of dramatic
art. He saw in theater what many literary critics could not: that
drama cannot be reduced to the literary. Applying concepts from
classical anthropology, he linked the study of ritual to the study of
drama. His perspective exercised great influence over later scholarship on the theater, especially in Shakespeare studies. The book
was and continues to be an excellent theoretical and analytical
guide to understanding dramatic form and dramatic ideas.

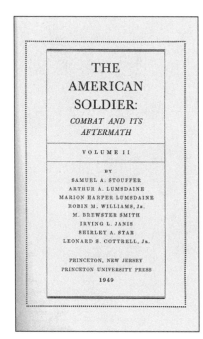

The American Soldier: Combat and Its Aftermath

1949

Samuel A. Stouffer, Arthur A. Lumsdaine, Marion Harper Lumsdaine, Robin M. Williams, Jr., M. Brewster Smith, Irving L. Janis, Shirley A. Star, and Leonard S. Cottrell, Jr.

*T*he American Soldier: Combat and Its Aftermath was the first comprehensive study ever undertaken of the attitudes of combat infantrymen in war. Working from large survey samples taken among infantrymen who fought in World War II, Samuel Stouffer and his associates presented the first data available on individual men's feelings about their performance and motivation in combat. This volume became the essential source of data on soldiers for scholars working in military, organizational, and social psychology.

Stouffer's study concluded that in World War II neither ideology nor patriotism was the major motivating factor for soldiers in combat. The main motivations were, rather, unity and the bonds soldiers formed with each other. Stouffer's work formed the basis for research into topics ranging from the moral dilemma of killing to how to enhance individual performance in military operations, and it is still cited today. At the time this book was published, the *New York Times* called the study "a monumental contribution to the science of making citizens of a free country win its wars."

This book was one of a four-volume set. The other volumes bore the subtitles *Adjustment during Army Life, Experiments on Mass Communication,* and *Measurement and Prediction. Combat and Its Aftermath* has been the most frequently cited among the volumes.

1950– The Papers of Thomas Jefferson

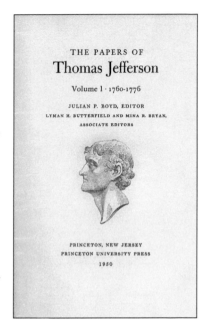

THE PAPERS OF
Thomas Jefferson
Volume 1 · 1760-1776

JULIAN P. BOYD, EDITOR
LYMAN H. BUTTERFIELD AND MINA R. BRYAN,
ASSOCIATE EDITORS

PRINCETON, NEW JERSEY
PRINCETON UNIVERSITY PRESS
1950

For more than five decades, the Press has been involved in some of the most ambitious endeavors in scholarly publishing—multivolume papers projects undertaken by large research teams at great expense and completed over many years. The first at Princeton was *The Papers of Thomas Jefferson*, under the editorship of university librarian and later Princeton professor of history Julian Boyd. Boyd conceived of the project in 1943 while serving on the Thomas Jefferson Bicentennial Commission. The project's goal was—and remains—to prepare an authoritative and comprehensive edition of the correspondence and papers of Jefferson. Current editor Barbara B. Oberg hopes to complete the project's remaining forty volumes by July 4, 2026, the bicentennial of Jefferson's death.

Upon publication of the first volume in 1950, the Jefferson Papers received a grand send-off at the Library of Congress in a ceremony presided over by President Truman. The project renewed interest in the nation's documentary heritage and set the standard for the organization and presentation of historical documents, so much so that the highest honor awarded today by the Association for Documentary Editing is named for Julian P. Boyd. It became the model for the papers of Franklin, Adams, Hamilton, Madison, Wilson, and others.

As part of the lavish attention the Press devoted to the project, Press designer P. J. Conkwright and the Mergenthaler Linotype Company spent nearly six years reinventing an eighteenth-century typeface, which they dubbed "Monticello," expressly for the Jefferson Papers.

P. J. Conkwright and Book Design

Throughout its history, Princeton University Press has produced consistently elegant books. Beginning with the hiring of respected book designer Frederic Warde in the 1920s, the Press has shown a strong commitment to the craft of book design. By the middle of the twentieth century, P. J. Conkwright, the legendary designer and typographer at Princeton, had sealed Princeton's reputation as a press with the highest design standards. Even as technology has evolved and working procedures have changed, the Press has maintained its ability to produce well-crafted books.

In his 1951 history of the Press, Whitney Darrow, the Press's founding director, describes the appreciation for the craft of book design that Charles Scribner had instilled in him. It was in 1921 that designer and typographer Frederic Warde was hired as the Press's first printing director. Before his arrival at Princeton, Warde had spent three years working with acclaimed designer Bruce Rogers at William E. Rudge's successful printing plant in Mount Vernon, New York.

Warde, a self-described perfectionist, created works that were classic in design and feel. As a result of underinking and a light impression, his pages were intentionally gray, light, and even. During his brief tenure, Warde jump-started Princeton University Press's program of quality design and printing.

Pleasant Jefferson ("P. J.") Conkwright joined the Press in 1939, coming from the University of Oklahoma. As the Press's chief designer and typographer from 1939 until 1970, Conkwright earned widespread recognition among both design and scholarly communities, transforming Princeton into a center of tasteful and innovative design. Working closely with the Press director and the production/plant manager, he promoted design principles that ensured a basic level of quality for all of Princeton's books. Believing that a book's design should contribute to the communication of the author's idea, Conkwright felt that any book should meet basic requirements for the reader: it should lie flat when opened, have margins wide enough to allow for a firm grip when held in the hands, possess a stamped spine that would be legible for many years, and display clear and readable type. He insisted that paper and binding materials be carefully selected, and he consistently argued for the best materials available within the project's budget. These principles continue to govern Princeton's book design and manufacturing.

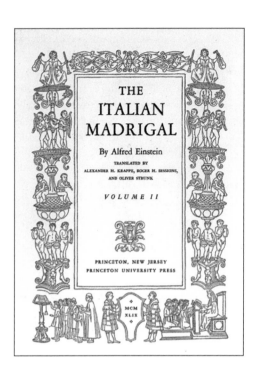

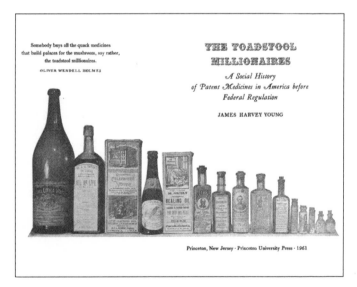

Two title pages by P. J. Conkwright: *The Italian Madrigal*, vol. 2, by Alfred Einstein (1949); *The Toadstool Millionaires*, by James Harvey Young (1961).

One of Conkwright's greatest skills was his ability to organize complicated scholarly material in a way that made it easier to use. The best-known example of his work is the collected writings of Thomas Jefferson (see illustration, p. 32). This colossal project involved the commissioning of a new Linotype typeface, Monticello, based on a historic typeface originally produced by the Philadelphia foundry Binny & Ronaldson. Conkwright paid special attention to materials as well, selecting a warm-toned laid sheet (textured paper) that he developed with the Curtis Paper Company. The sense of elegance and decorum in Conkwright's series design was widely recognized, and *The Papers of Thomas Jefferson* quickly became a model for historical papers published by other university presses. Conkwright's other major works for the Press include *The Papers of Woodrow Wilson, The Writings of Henry D. Thoreau*, and Charles De Tolnay's five-volume *Michelangelo*.

In addition to his focus on craft, Conkwright had a strong sense of community. He had an ongoing relationship with the Princeton University library, designing the *Library Chronicle*, its special collection bookplates, and its exhibition catalogs. Conkwright also designed for professors, alumni, and administrators through the printing division that was then a part of Princeton University Press.

Many designers who worked with Conkwright have received significant recognition within the American university press community, most notably Helen van Zandt, Jan Lilly, and Frank Mahood. Van Zandt, Conkwright's assistant beginning in 1945, was listed as designer along with Conkwright on many of his design awards.

Trained under Conkwright and van Zandt, Jan Lilly joined the Press full-time in 1966 as an apprentice book designer, eventually rising to design department manager. She is a widely respected designer, whose work is characterized by a subtle elegance and typographic sophistication. She has won multiple awards from the American Association of University Presses (AAUP), the American Institute of Graphic Arts (AIGA), and the New York book shows. Most recently, she has been praised for her handling of the *Barrington Atlas* (see p. 154), described by the judges at the 2001 Book, Jacket, and Journal Show, organized by the AAUP, as "the atlas to die for. The eleven-year effort was worth it. Masterful."

Conkwright also hired Frank Mahood in 1968. While Mahood works in a broad range of styles, he is best known for his extraordinary use of ornament and decorative elements. His attention to detail and his ability to use multiple elements in harmonious ways have earned him many design awards from the AAUP and the AIGA. In 2002 a small book of poetry, *Music of a Distant Drum*, designed by Mahood was described in the 2002 AAUP Book, Jacket, and Journal Show as "a lovely little book" and "utterly suitable and engaging." His work as a book designer and illustrator was featured in an exhibition at Princeton University's Firestone Library.

The Press produces more than two hundred new hardcovers and ninety new paperbacks each year; almost all are designed in-house. Although the Princeton list is larger and more complex than ever before—ranging from econometrics textbooks to volumes of poetry, from field guides to scholarly monographs—the Press has continually been recognized not only for text design but also for high-quality cover and jacket design, winning fifteen awards in the past two years alone. The current designers exhibit an impressive range of styles, using traditional typographic approaches while embracing more experimental methods.

Nietzsche: *1950*

Philosopher,

Psychologist,

Antichrist

Walter Kaufmann

This classic is the benchmark against which all modern books about Nietzsche are measured. When Walter Kaufmann wrote it in the immediate aftermath of World War II, most scholars outside Germany viewed Nietzsche as part madman, part proto-Nazi, and almost wholly unphilosophical. Kaufmann rehabilitated Nietzsche nearly single-handedly, presenting his works as one of the great achievements of Western philosophy.

Responding to the powerful myths and countermyths that had sprung up around Nietzsche, Kaufmann offered a patient, even-handed account of his life and works, and of the uses and abuses to which subsequent generations had put his ideas. Without ignoring or downplaying the ugliness of many of Nietzsche's proclamations, he set them in the context of his work as a whole and of the counterexamples yielded by a responsible reading of his books. More positively, he presented Nietzsche's ideas about power as one of the great accomplishments of modern philosophy, arguing that his conception of the "will to power" was not a crude apology for ruthless self-assertion but must be linked to Nietzsche's equally profound ideas about sublimation. He also presented Nietzsche as a pioneer of modern psychology and argued that a key to understanding his overall philosophy is to see it as a reaction against Christianity.

Many scholars in the past half century have taken issue with some of Kaufmann's interpretations, but the book ranks as one of the most influential accounts ever written of any major Western thinker.

1950 Ancient Near Eastern Texts Relating to the Old Testament

James Bennett Pritchard

ANCIENT
NEAR EASTERN
TEXTS

RELATING TO
THE OLD TESTAMENT

EDITED BY JAMES B. PRITCHARD

PRINCETON, NEW JERSEY
PRINCETON UNIVERSITY PRESS
1950

This anthology brought together the most important historical, legal, mythological, liturgical, and secular texts of the ancient Near East, with the purpose of providing a rich contextual base for understanding the people, cultures, and literature of the Old Testament. A scholar of religious thought and biblical archaeology, James Pritchard recruited the foremost linguists, historians, and archaeologists to select and translate the texts. The goal, in his words, was "a better understanding of the likenesses and differences which existed between Israel and the surrounding cultures." Before the publication of these volumes, students of the Old Testament found themselves having to search out scattered books and journals in various languages. This anthology brought these invaluable documents together, in one place and in one language, thereby expanding the meaning and significance of the Bible for generations of students and readers. As one reviewer put it, "This great volume is one of the most notable to have appeared in the field of Old Testament scholarship this century."

Princeton published a follow-up companion volume, *The Ancient Near East in Pictures Relating to the Old Testament* (1954), and later a one-volume abridgment of the two, *The Ancient Near East: An Anthology of Texts and Pictures* (1958). The continued popularity of this work in its various forms demonstrates that anthologies have a very important role to play in education—and in the mission of a university press.

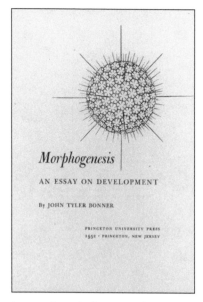

Morphogenesis   *1952*

An Essay on

Development

John Tyler Bonner

By profession, John Bonner is a developmental biologist who has spent most of his career studying cellular slime molds. By vocation, he is a superb science essayist in the tradition of Lewis Thomas and Stephen Jay Gould. An extraordinarily innovative mind, Bonner has opened up new fields of intellectual exploration: the evolution of complexity, the relationship between evolution and development, the role of size in organisms, and beyond. Since publishing *Morphogenesis* with the Press, he has written eight more books for Princeton including *Size and Cycle* (1965), *The Evolution of Culture in Animals* (1980), and *The Evolution of Complexity by Means of Natural Selection* (1988). This oeuvre represents a major intellectual landmark.

A Bonner book is likely to range widely across biology, from animal communication to the fossil record to the molecular biology of development. Even as biologists around him broke up into sparring departments of ecology and evolution, molecular biology, and genetics, John Bonner keeps his eye on the whole field. Second, it is focused on some of the major questions in biology. Why did life become multicellular? Why are some organisms big and some small? How do processes at the molecular and cellular levels relate to larger behavioral and ecological dynamics? Third, it is written in a style that is neither popular science nor professional monograph. Bonner assumes little knowledge, he explains every concept in simple terms, and yet he builds up intellectually sophisticated arguments that move an area of inquiry to a new level.

1953 *Mimesis: The Representation of Reality in Western Literature*

Erich Auerbach

Translated from the German

A half century after its translation into English, Erich Auerbach's *Mimesis* still stands as a monumental achievement in literary criticism. A brilliant display of erudition, wit, and wisdom, his exploration of how great European writers from Homer to Virginia Woolf depicted everyday reality has taught generations how to read Western literature.

A German Jew, Auerbach was forced out of his professorship at the University of Marburg in 1935. He left for Turkey, where he taught at the state university in Istanbul. There he wrote *Mimesis*, publishing it in German after the end of the war. Displaced as he was, Auerbach produced a work of great erudition that contains no footnotes, basing his arguments instead on searching, illuminating readings of key passages from his primary texts. His aim was to show how from antiquity to the twentieth century literature progressed toward ever more naturalistic and democratic forms of representation. This essentially optimistic view of European history now appears as a defensive—and impassioned—response to the inhumanity he saw in the Third Reich. Ranging over works in Greek, Latin, Spanish, French, Italian, German, and English, Auerbach used his remarkable skills in philology and comparative literature to refute any narrow form of nationalism or chauvinism, in his own day and ours.

For many readers, both inside and outside the academy, *Mimesis* is among the finest works of literary criticism ever written.

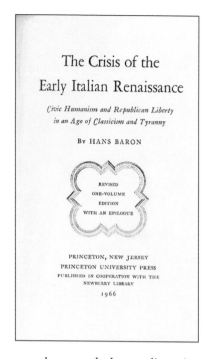

The Crisis of the
Early Italian Renaissance

*Civic Humanism and Republican Liberty
in an Age of Classicism and Tyranny*

By HANS BARON

REVISED
ONE-VOLUME
EDITION
WITH AN EPILOGUE

PRINCETON, NEW JERSEY
PRINCETON UNIVERSITY PRESS
PUBLISHED IN COOPERATION WITH THE
NEWBERRY LIBRARY
1966

*Italian Renaissance:
Civic Humanism and
Republican Liberty
in an Age of Classi-
cism and Tyranny
(two volumes)*

Hans Baron

Hans Baron was one of the many great German émigré scholars whose work Princeton brought into the Anglo-American world. His *Crisis of the Early Italian Renais-sance* has provoked more discussion and inspired more research than any other twentieth-century study of the Italian Renaissance.

Baron's book was the first historical synthesis of politics and humanism at that momentous critical juncture when Italy passed from medievalism to the thought of the Renaissance. Baron, un-like his peers, married culture and politics; he contended that to truly understand the Renaissance one must understand the rise of humanism within the political context of the day. This marked a significant departure for the field and one that changed the direc-tion of Renaissance studies. Moreover, Baron's book was one of the first major attempts of any sort to ground intellectual history in a fully realized historical context and thus stands at the very origins of the interdisciplinary approach that is now the core of Renaissance studies.

Baron's analysis of the forces that changed life and thought in fifteenth-century Italy was widely reviewed domestically and inter-nationally, and scholars quickly noted that the book "will hence-forth be the starting point for any general discussion of the early Renaissance." The *Times Literary Supplement* called it "a model of the kind of intensive study on which all understanding of cultural process must rest." First published in 1955 in two volumes, the work was reissued in a one-volume Princeton edition in 1966.

History, Politics, and Culture

Anthony Grafton

In 1990, Princeton University Press published a slender book by one of its longtime authors, Felix Gilbert: *History: Politics or Culture? Reflections on Ranke and Burckhardt.* This learned and eloquent study of two of the nineteenth century's greatest historians, Leopold von Ranke and Jacob Burckhardt, sums up many of the Press's accomplishments in two of its central fields. Gilbert was one of the many distinguished European émigrés whose work appeared on the Press's list in the second half of the twentieth century, transforming American scholarship. A scion of the Mendelssohn family of Berlin, he studied history there with Friedrich Meinecke. Coming to America in the 1930s, he worked in the OSS during World War II, taught at Bryn Mawr, and eventually became a professor in the School of Historical Studies at the Institute for Advanced Study in Princeton.

Though Gilbert never formally sponsored a doctoral dissertation, he inspired many younger students of the Italian Renaissance with his mastery of both archival sources, which he had studied intensively in Italy since the 1930s, and textual analysis. His own scholarship transformed the study of political and historical thought in the High Renaissance, the age of Machiavelli and Guicciardini, as he rooted the texts in the institutions in which their authors served, the crisis of the Italian Wars through which they lived, and the language of the political and social elite, which Gilbert reconstructed from archival records of their debates. A preeminent cultural historian, he taught generations of specialists in the Renaissance that they would impoverish it if they ignored politics, economics, and warfare. At the end of Gilbert's life, when he returned to two master historians of the modern German tradition, one of whom had studied with the other, he dedicated his packed, concise essay to the big question their work posed: should history concentrate on the state, the great organizing force in history, and on its efforts to shape society by making laws and waging wars, or on culture, the rich tapestry of meanings woven by ordinary men and women, not only through art and literature but also through manners, rituals, and clothing?

Gilbert, as his wonderfully fluent but heavily accented English made clear, was a European, the product of a culture and an academic system radically different from the American. He saw most things—including American military and foreign policy, on which he wrote an important book—from a distinctive, non-American point of view. At Princeton University Press, however, his work marked not an exception but one among many examples of a characteristic style. Though Princeton University Press has always been connected to a great university, it has also always been open to the wider perspectives of scholars from other countries and traditions. The origins of this tradition go back as far as 1925, when the Press published Henri Pirenne's *Medieval Cities*. But its real heyday, which has never quite ended, began with the rise of the Nazis and the Second World War. Hitler shook the trees, to adapt a metaphor first applied to art history, and the Press caught the apples. A generation of European scholars, expelled from their homes and deprived of their careers, found new places in the American university. Princeton University Press became one of their preferred publishers—and after it took over Bollingen Series, perhaps their favorite.

The histories these scholars wrote ranged widely in scale and period—from the erudite, tightly structured studies of Gilbert and Hans Baron, sharply focused on a few decades in the history of the Italian Renaissance, through the sprawling books of Ernst Kantorowicz and Richard Krautheimer, which spanned the medieval centuries, to the work of Siegfried Kracauer and others on modern European and American culture. But all of them were linked—linked, first of all, by an erudition founded in the great European secondary schools and universities that Erwin Panofsky described, in an essay first published by the Press; linked again by long years of scholarly apprenticeship; and linked, a third time, by the need to make their findings accessible to an English-speaking public. Princeton University Press, with its traditions of fine book design, its passionate concern for craftsmanship and accuracy, and its openness to new forms of scholarship, brought this new intellectual style into the Anglo-American world.

At the same time, the Press offered opportunities to the most original American scholars to bring their own distinctive approaches to European history. Princeton University Press enabled Ira Wade and R. R. Palmer, for example, to bring out pathbreaking studies of the Enlightenment, rooted in new research methods, before World War II, and encouraged both to attack wider problems and reach larger audiences after the war. The Press also published Joseph Strayer's distinctive inquiries, both monographic and comparative, into the medieval state; Jerome Blum's pioneering investigations into the lives and fates of peasants, from Russia to Western Europe; and Charles Gillispie's challenging synthetic history of the long trajectory of Western science as well as his richly particular monographs on French science and its larger eighteenth- and nineteenth-century context. A small press in New Jersey became the site where European history, medieval, early modern, and modern, was renewed, over and over again. The Press remained hospitable as a generation of younger American scholars, many of them the students of the émigrés—Robert Benson and Robert Brentano in medieval studies; Gene Brucker, Lauro Martines, and Donald Weinstein in the Renaissance; Theodore von Laue, Charles Maier, and Jerrold Seigel in modern history—developed their own new styles of inquiry into the European past. At the same time, the Press also continued to welcome the results of foreign scholarship. It was a hospitable venue for the New Zealand–born, British-educated, and absolutely individualist historian John Pocock, for the publication of his comprehensive revisionist history of republican thought in Europe and the United States, which reoriented the discussions of historians and political theorists as dramatically as Hans Baron had done a generation before.

The questions Gilbert addressed in his last book, moreover, were central to the Press's authors over the decades. Princeton University Press has always dedicated close attention to the state, which for Gilbert constituted the central object of serious historical and political thought. From Edward Corwin, whose great study of the American Constitution first appeared in 1920, onward, original students of political and constitutional thought have made the Press their natural home. Over the generations, their methods and concerns have changed, as new analytical methods came into play. The interpretation of texts has been enriched both by new approaches to the relations between political thinkers and the state—the subject of a groundbreaking book by Nannerl Keohane—and by new hermeneutical methods, many of them devised by Quentin Skinner and debated in a rich volume edited by James Tully.

Like Gilbert, an impenitent admirer of Ranke, those who have written about the state for Princeton University Press have taken at least as much interest in the institutions and day-to-day practices of government as in its theoretical foundations. Medieval historians from Joseph Strayer to William Chester Jordan have traced the development of central Western institutions, from legal systems to tax offices, over the centuries. Political scientists have made the Press a center of innovation in their field. Princeton produced most of Robert Gilpin's many pioneering studies on the economic context of international relations and on the relations between science and the state. It published both *Small Groups and Political Behavior*, the book with which Sidney Verba began his long career as a specialist in political participation and citizenship, and *The Civic Culture*, in which Verba and Gabriel Almond, focusing in a precise, comparative way on the citizens of five democracies, transformed the study of democracies and how they come into being. Studies of participation and civic behavior remained a central concern for the Press. In 1993 it brought out Robert Putnam's acclaimed analysis of Italian civic institutions, *Making Democracy Work*—a monographic study with major implications, which has spawned an immense progeny of political and social commentary. From the Cold War to the present era of globalization, specialists in international relations like George Kennan, Robert Keohane, and Richard Falk have drawn attention to the changing nature of world politics and have kept the larger political contexts of diplomacy at the center of the Press's concerns. No one, perhaps, has done more to shape discussion in this field than the historian Edward Muir and the anthropologist Clifford Geertz, whose studies of ritual politics in Renaissance Venice and nineteenth-century Bali focused the attention of scholars across the humanities and social sciences on the multiple ways in which public ceremonies shaped—and shape—the relations between governments and the governed.

Ranke and Burckhardt both knew that all governments are rooted in particular social worlds, and both set themselves to explain how laws and institutions took shape in particular social and economic circumstances. Over the decades, the Press has sponsored a vast set of inquiries into the larger history of society and its relation to politics. John Franklin Jameson, one of the founders of professional history in the United States, delivered at Princeton the series of lectures that the Press published as *The American Revolution Considered as a Social Movement*. This essay of 1926, which insisted that the social divisions within Revolutionary America had been in some ways sharper than the split between the colonies and England, was the harbinger of a vast array of inquiries into everything from the demographic foundations of modern society—later explored in a massive series of monographs organized and edited by the Princeton demographer Ansley Coale—to the social histories of Western and non-Western societies. Early in the 1960s, Lee Benson brought the new social history, based on quantitative study of groups and their behavior, to bear on the development of Jacksonian democracy—and used it to argue, in the teeth of interpretations that went back to the revisionist histories of Charles Beard, that economic status had not determined the ways in which Americans voted. Later, the Press published William Aydelotte's pioneering quantitative analysis of the British House of Commons.

Princeton's tradition in politics, as in history, has been eclectic. Rather than specializing in quantitative or qualitative approaches, it brought out a celebrated interdisciplinary work by Gary King, Robert Keohane, and Sidney Verba, *Designing Social Inquiry*, which teases out the common logic of social inquiry that links the two sets of approaches. The Press has produced both powerful monographs, like Putnam's study of Italy, and wide-ranging comparative studies, like Jeffrey Herbst's *States and Power in Africa . . .* And it has warmly encouraged efforts to draw tools from other disciplines and apply them to the study of politics—as in Robert Jervis's groundbreaking *Perception and Misperception in International Politics* (1976), which used cognitive psychology to elucidate the ways in which decision makers read and misread history.

Ranke and Burckhardt knew that many forces shaped societies and states. Religion, for example, was central to the history of the modern West. And religion—considered from every point of view, from institutions and theology to ritual and religious art— has always been at the core of the Press's interests. In the 1960s, medievalists like Robert Brentano and Robert Benson published with the Press what remain classic studies of the institutions of medieval Catholicism. Students of the Reformation, such as Horton Davies, and of the French Revolution, such as Timothy Tackett, pursued similar themes into later centuries. Tightly focused, dazzlingly written studies by Mark Pegg, Jeffrey Freedman, and Brendan Dooley have kept the institutional history of Christian churches at the very center of the Press's offerings in European history. Jewish history—which the Press entered with a splash in 1973, when it published Gershom Scholem's extraordinary study of Sabbatai Sevi and his followers—has become one of its special interests. Amos Funkenstein's *Theology and the Scientific Imagination*, for example, brilliantly traced remarkable and little-known connections between the greatest Jewish thinker of the Middle Ages, Maimonides, and the founders of the seventeenth-century New Philosophy. A whole series of recent monographs by Mark Cohen, Susan Einbinder, and others have pursued this interest into new sources and periods. Meanwhile learned and subtle studies by David Frankfurter and Seth Schwartz have tracked relations between Christianity and rival religions backward into one of the most fertile areas of all—the study of late antiquity, a field largely inspired by the Princeton historian Peter Brown.

Like Gilbert's heroes, the Press's authors have always been willing to break new ground. For almost half a century, for example, the Press has been a major publisher of work in the relatively new discipline of history of science. From Gillispie's *The Edge of Objectivity*, a pioneering work of synthesis, through his own later work on science in eighteenth- and nineteenth-century France, the Press has pursued closely textured studies of modern science and the larger contexts—religious, political, institutional—in which it took shape. During this period, the history of science has developed multiple approaches to its endlessly varied object. Methods used in the field range from tight, internal study of individual scientific projects and writings to richly detailed, microhistorical accounts of the social and material worlds in which investigators and authors worked. The Press has followed every one of these branching trails. Its offerings have spanned the continuum from the precise and demanding studies of Kepler by Bruce Stephenson and James Voelkel to the deeply detailed, almost archaeological study of individual scientists and their work practiced by Steven Shapin and Simon Schaffer in *Leviathan and the Air-Pump* and Gerald Geison in *The Private Science of Louis Pasteur*. Some of the Press's most innovative and influential products have been devoted to traditions of thought about nature that now lie entirely outside the world of scientific practice—as traced over the long term in William Eamon's massive study of books of secrets and crystallized in microscopic form in Ann Blair's pathbreaking book on Jean Bodin.

Ranke and Burckhardt both understood—as some more recent professional scholars have not—that warfare and violence form a central theme in both politics and history, with its own forms and its own cultures. The Press has shown a clear understanding of this point as well. Its publications run the gamut, from classic studies of decision-making elites by Edward Meade Earle and Richard Challener, through Peter Paret's penetrating analyses of Clausewitz and his place in the history of military thought, to the collective studies of Vietnam and international law organized by Richard Falk, and the fearless analysis of civil violence during wartime by the political scientist Jan Gross, *Neighbors*. In maintaining this tradition, the Press has contributed to the political education of a readership that proved all too ready to believe, as the twentieth century came to an end, that warfare was ceasing to be a central concern of governments and their advisers.

Ranke and Burckhardt—and Gilbert—were adepts of technical scholarship, but they were also great stylists, who set out to address and educate a broad cultured public. The Press—as Gross's case suggests—has always been willing to do the same. Works like Robert Palmer's best-selling *Twelve Who Ruled*, Pietro Redondi's *Galileo Heretic*, and Gross's *Neighbors* have reached tens of thousands of readers, acquainting them with the results of professional scholarship in highly accessible forms. Many other Press books—like Corwin's study of the Constitution and Blum's work on Russian social history—have become durable textbooks, used by thousands of students over the generations. Studies of "public intellectuals" in the United States have tended to concentrate on the magazines in which professional scholars set out to address a wider public. In its own way, however, Princeton University Press—with its policy of encouraging authors to combine monographic studies with synthesis, its ability to edit and market books of both kinds, and its consistently high reputation in the academy—has contributed as much as any generalist periodical to informing and provoking a wide public.

The Press's long tradition of openness to new questions and new methods has occasionally given rise to problems. A few books have revealed serious flaws when exposed to systematic criticism, while others, though praised by the reviewers, have not immediately found a large audience. But no publisher willing to attack new subjects can avoid these risks. On the whole, the Press has succeeded, to an astonishing extent, in preserving into the current age of new production methods and high competitive pressures the standards set half a century ago and more, when writers and editors agreed that it was worth spending years on editing and production.

At a time when outside critics of the academy rant on and on about the politicization of scholarship, the hegemony of jargon, and the abandonment of standards, the Press has maintained a great tradition in history and politics. Its editors and advisers have managed to combine broad interests, a focus on questions of public as well as intellectual concern, and a willingness to take chances with an absolute commitment to rigorous refereeing, precise editing and printing, and handsome, distinctive design.

Felix Gilbert—whose scholarship was characterized by all of these qualities—would undoubtedly be as pleased by the newer company in which his Princeton books appear as he was by their older companions.

Anthony Grafton is the Henry Putnam University Professor of History at Princeton University, where he teaches the cultural history of Renaissance Europe, the history of books and readers, the history of scholarship and education in the West from antiquity to the nineteenth century, and the history of science from antiquity to the Renaissance. He is a longtime friend of the Press and served on the Press's editorial board from January 1988 to December 1993.

Henri Cartan and Samuel Eilenberg

H enri Cartan and Sam-
uel Eilenberg first
met in 1947 in New York,
and an intellectual collaboration and friendship ensued. They spent five years
writing this book together
between meetings in Paris
and New York. The man-
uscript acquired the nick-
name "Diplodocus," after
the dinosaur of the same
name, because it was so
large. Many people, unable to wait for the book, made use of Cartan and Eilenberg's draft notes. The eventual outcome of their
collaboration was *Homological Algebra*, in which the authors tied
together strands of algebra and topology to create the new mathematical field named in the book's title. Homological algebra is
an area of mathematics in which the techniques of topology are
applied to the structure of algebra.

For more than forty years this book has been considered the
primary reference for homological algebra. Not only did it develop an entirely new field, it also provided the tools for the development of modern algebraic geometry. In the decade leading
up to the book's publication, the methods of algebraic topology
had invaded the domain of pure algebra and initiated a number
of internal revolutions. The purpose of this book was to present a
unified account of these developments and to lay the foundations
of a full-fledged theory of algebraic topology.

Both Cartan and Eilenberg won the prestigious Wolf Prize, established in 1978 to honor scientists who promote science that
benefits humankind. Eilenberg wrote, with Norman Steenrod,
Foundations of Algebraic Topology (Princeton, 1952), which also
remains a primary work in the field.

1956 Soviet-American Relations, 1917–1920, Volume 1: *Russia Leaves the War*

George F. Kennan

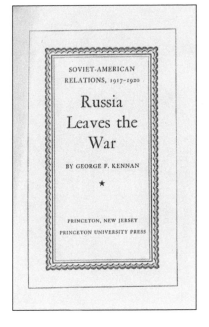

Winner of the National Book Award and the Pulitzer, Bancroft, and Parkman Prizes, George Kennan's *Russia Leaves the War* explored the complexities of the Soviet-American relationship between November 1917 and March 1918. These four months, which witnessed the Bolshevik Revolution and Russia's departure from the warring powers, set the stage for future relations between the two emerging superpowers. Volume 2 of *Soviet American Relations*, entitled *The Decision to Intervene* (Princeton, 1958), explored U.S. intervention in northern Russia and Siberia between 1918 and 1920. Ultimately, the distinguished diplomat and former ambassador to Russia provided a vivid portrait of the personal and social factors that shaped American policy toward the Soviet Union and communism as a whole.

Kennan became the U.S. government's key analyst of the Soviet Union after a two-year stint in the Foreign Service there (1944–1946), which had been preceded by service in the American embassy in Moscow before World War II. His "long telegram" to his superiors at the State Department, written in 1946 and published a year later in revised form in *Foreign Affairs* as the famous "X" article, was perhaps the most influential statement in the early years of the Cold War.

After leaving the Foreign Service, Kennan joined the faculty at the School for Historical Studies at the Institute for Advanced Study in Princeton, where he wrote *Russia Leaves the War* and subsequent books.

Anatomy of Criticism: **1957**
Four Essays

Northrop Frye

Here is a book fundamental
enough to be entitled
Principia Critica.

—Commonweal

Northrop Frye was one of the most important and influential literary theorists of the twentieth century, and *Anatomy of Criticism* is his magnum opus. More than any other North American critic, Frye paved the way for the explosion of interest in literary theory that took hold in the 1960s. Breaking with the practice of close readings of individual texts, favored by the so-called New Critics before him, Frye argued that literary study should be scientific in nature, not merely impressionistic or personal. "What critics now have," as he put it in one of many incisive formulations, "is a mystery-religion without a gospel, and they are initiates who can communicate, or quarrel, only with one another."

Frye sought instead to give us a common basis for understanding the full range of literary forms, through a far-reaching but integrated series of essays on literary archetypes, genres, poetic language, and the relations among text, reader, and society at large. Using a dazzling array of examples—from the *Odyssey* to *The Tale of Genji* to *The Water-Babies*—he argued that understanding "the structure of literature as a total form" allows us to see the profoundly liberating effect that literature can have in freeing our imaginations from the constraints of habit and circumstance.

Princeton also published Frye's first book, *Fearful Symmetry* (1947), his masterful study of William Blake's visionary symbolism.

1957 *Banks and Politics in America from the Revolution to the Civil War*

Bray Hammond

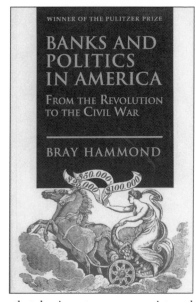

"This is a book about politics and banks and history. Yet politicians who read it will see that the author is not a politician, bankers who read it will see that he is not a banker, and historians that he is not an historian. Economists will see that he is not an economist and lawyers that he is not a lawyer."

With this rather cryptic and exhaustive disclaimer, Bray Hammond began his classic investigation into the role of banking in the formation of American society. Hammond, who was assistant secretary of the Board of Governors of the Federal Reserve System from 1944 to 1950, presented in this 771-page book the definitive account of how banking evolved in the United States in the context of the nation's political and social development.

Hammond combined political with financial analysis, highlighting not only the influence politicians exercised over banking but also how banking drove political interests and created political coalitions. He captured the entrepreneurial, expansive, risk-taking spirit of the United States from earliest days and then showed how that spirit sometimes undermined sound banking institutions. In Hammond's view, we need central banks to keep the economy on an even keel. Historian Richard Sylla judged the work to be "a wry and urbane study of early U.S. financial history, but also a timeless essay on how Americans became what they are." *Banks and Politics in America* won the Pulitzer Prize for history in 1958.

THE KING'S
TWO BODIES
A Study in
Mediaeval Political Theology

BY

ERNST H. KANTOROWICZ

PRINCETON, NEW JERSEY
PRINCETON UNIVERSITY PRESS
1957

The King's Two Bodies: A Study in Mediaeval Political Theology

Ernst H. Kantorowicz

Medieval historian Ernst Kantorowicz's masterpiece describes how medieval and Renaissance thinkers devised a complex and, at times, mystical continuity between kingship and the person who happened to hold the office. This continuity was theorized as the "king's two bodies." The king's natural body has physical attributes, suffers, and dies, naturally, as do all humans; but the king's other body, the spiritual body, transcends the earthly and serves as a symbol of his office as majesty with the divine right to rule. The notion of the two bodies allowed for the continuity of monarchy even when the monarch died, as summed up in the formulation "The king is dead. Long live the king."

Bringing together liturgical works, images, and polemical material, *The King's Two Bodies* explores the long Christian past behind this "political theology." It provides a subtle history of how commonwealths developed symbolic means for establishing their sovereignty and, with such means, began to establish early forms of the nation-state.

Kantorowicz fled Nazi Germany in 1938, after refusing to sign a Nazi loyalty oath, and settled in the United States. While teaching at the University of California, Berkeley, he once again refused to sign an oath of allegiance, this one designed to identify Communist Party sympathizers. He resigned as a result of the controversy and moved to the Institute for Advanced Study in Princeton, where he remained for the rest of his life, and where he wrote *The King's Two Bodies*.

1958 The Society of Captives: A Study of a Maximum Security Prison

Gresham M. Sykes

THE SOCIETY OF CAPTIVES

A STUDY OF A

MAXIMUM SECURITY PRISON

BY GRESHAM M. SYKES

The Society of Captives is one of the most important books ever written about prison as well as a startlingly original contribution to our thinking about punishment and social control in general. The book transformed how we understand the psychological and organizational dynamics of prison life, and has become a classic of modern criminology.

Gresham Sykes wrote the book at the height of the Cold War, motivated by the world's experience of fascism and communism to study the closest thing to a totalitarian system in American life: a maximum security prison. The book is remarkably short—just 150 pages—but bristles with ideas. Sykes argued that many of the psychological effects of modern prison are even more brutal than the physical cruelties of the past. The trauma of being designated one of the very worst human beings in the world left prisoners with lifelong scars. It also inspired solidarity among prisoners and fierce resistance to authorities as strategies for rejecting those who rejected them. His analysis called into question whether prisons genuinely were, as many believed, "total institutions," where every facet of life was rigidly controlled. Sykes showed that the stronger the bonds among prisoners, the more difficult it was for prison guards to run the prisons without finding ways of "accommodating" the prisoners.

The book set the stage for Michel Foucault's *Discipline and Punish*, among other works. Since it appeared in 1958, it has served society as an indispensable text in coming to terms with the nature of modern power.

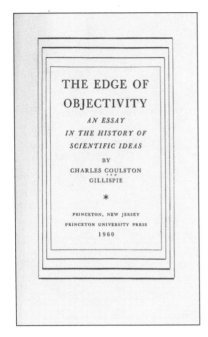

THE EDGE OF
OBJECTIVITY

AN ESSAY
IN THE HISTORY OF
SCIENTIFIC IDEAS

BY
CHARLES COULSTON
GILLISPIE

*

PRINCETON, NEW JERSEY
PRINCETON UNIVERSITY PRESS
1960

The Edge of Objectivity: An Essay in the History of Scientific Ideas

1960

Charles Coulston Gillispie

In the mid-1950s, a young professor at Princeton named Charles Gillispie began teaching Humanities 304, one of the first undergraduate courses offered anywhere in the world on the history of science. From start to finish—Galileo to Einstein—Gillispie introduced the students to the key ideas and individuals in science. *The Edge of Objectivity* arose out of this course.

It must have been a lively class. *The Edge of Objectivity* is pointed, opinionated, and selective. Even at six hundred pages, the book is, as the title suggests, an essay. Gillispie is unafraid to rate Mendel higher than Darwin, Maxwell above Faraday. Full of wry turns of phrase, the book effectively captures people and places. And throughout the book, Gillispie pushes an argument. He views science as the progressive development of more objective, detached, mathematical ways of viewing the world, and he orchestrates his characters and ideas around this theme.

In the forty-five years since the publication of *The Edge of Objectivity*, historians of science have established a full-fledged discipline. They have focused increasingly on the social context of science rather than its internal dynamics, and they have frequently viewed science more as a threatening instance of power than as an accumulation of knowledge. Nevertheless, Gillispie's book remains a sophisticated, fast-moving, idiosyncratic account of the development of scientific ideas over four hundred years, by one of the founding intellects in the history of science.

1961 *The Concept*
of Jacksonian
Democracy:
New York
as a Test Case

Lee Benson

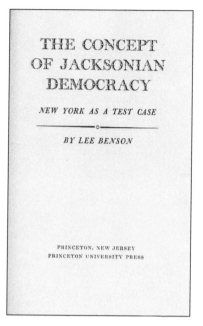

THE CONCEPT
OF JACKSONIAN
DEMOCRACY

NEW YORK AS A TEST CASE

BY LEE BENSON

PRINCETON, NEW JERSEY
PRINCETON UNIVERSITY PRESS

Historian Lee Benson was a key figure in the "new political history"—the attempt to apply social-science methods, concepts, and theories to American political history—and *The Concept of Jacksonian Democracy,* his pioneering study of nineteenth-century New York State political culture, was a major breakthrough in the field. One reviewer demanded that "every American political historian take cognizance of Benson's challenges," while another said the book "merited the attention of all political historians."

Benson challenged the very notion of a "Jacksonian" democracy, calling the concept "sterile and deceptive." Previous work, including that of Arthur Schlesinger, Jr., argued that voters cast their ballots according to economic status—rich for one party and poor for another. Benson's work turned this interpretation on its head. Using extensive quantitative research, he argued that ethnic and religious affiliations—not simply economic status—were the crucial determinants of political affiliation. Ethnocultural groups, as he called them, were often hostile to one another on the basis of prejudice or, more exactly, different lifestyle. Roman Catholics distrusted Protestants and vice versa, and each group tried to use its voting power to block the other's and enhance its own position. Calling previous interpretations "untenable," Benson argued that it was incorrect to understand voter behavior along strictly socioeconomic lines; the poor were no more likely to be Jacksonian Democrats than were the rich. In short, Benson suggested a new theory of American voting behavior.

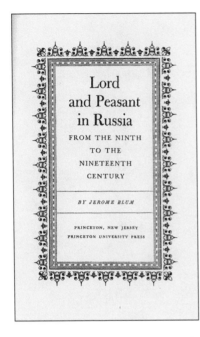

Jerome Blum

To understand Russian history without understanding serfdom—the peasant-lord relationship that shaped Russia for centuries—is impossible. Still, before Jerome Blum, no scholar had tackled the subject in depth. Monumental in scope and pathbreaking in its analysis, *Lord and Peasant in Russia* garnered immediate attention upon its publication in 1961, a year that also marked the one hundredth anniversary of the emancipation of the Russian serfs. As one reviewer remarked, "No better book on the subject exists; it is indispensable to the serious student of Russia."

On a scale befitting Russia—a sixth of the earth's land mass—Blum's book explored in almost seven hundred pages the legal and social evolution of its predominantly agricultural population, the types of peasant status, and the multifaceted nature of the master-peasant relationship. More important, Blum was the first to articulate the necessity of placing serfs front and center in the study of Russian history. As a reviewer for the *Economist* wrote, "Mr. Blum has written not just a monograph on landlords and peasants in Russia but a history of Russia from a particular point of view. There is no denying that the history of a country where . . . a bare 13 percent of the population was urban can with impunity be written in terms of landlords and peasants." In 1962, it was awarded the Herbert Baxter Adams Prize of the American Historical Association; it remains a cornerstone of Russian historiography.

1962 *Washington: Village and Capital, 1800–1878*

Constance McLaughlin Green

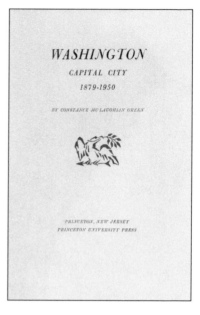

WASHINGTON

CAPITAL CITY

1879–1950

BY CONSTANCE MC LAUGHLIN GREEN

PRINCETON, NEW JERSEY
PRINCETON UNIVERSITY PRESS

Winner of the 1963 Pulitzer Prize in History, Constance McLaughlin Green's history of Washington, D.C., remains the most comprehensive history of the city. Green wrote her sweeping history in two volumes: *Washington: Village and Capital, 1800–1878* and *Washington: Capital City, 1879–1950*, published the following year. Despite stopping at 1950, the two volumes are still considered the standard work on the subject. Green described what made Washington unique—the constant presence of politics, the lack of representation in Congress, and the prominent role of African Americans in city life—as well as what made it like other American cities: crime, a desire to improve public education, suburbanization, and population growth. For, as Green wrote, "These strands of the unique, the distinctive, and the universal interweave to form the fabric of Washington's history."

Specifically, she examined real estate tendencies, race relations, business interests, and the role of public schools in the District. Still, in exploring the bureaucratic workings of the capital, Green never lost sight of Washington as a national symbol and source of national feeling—a city where, in the author's words, visitors rarely "failed to experience an emotional response compounded by pride, pleasure, dismay, anger, and an intense interest in the future."

Green served as head of the Washington History Project administered by American University. She wrote a third, follow-up volume to these two entitled *The Secret City: A History of Race Relations in the Nation's Capital* (Princeton, 1967).

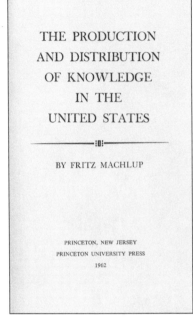

THE PRODUCTION
AND DISTRIBUTION
OF KNOWLEDGE
IN THE
UNITED STATES

BY FRITZ MACHLUP

PRINCETON, NEW JERSEY
PRINCETON UNIVERSITY PRESS
1962

The Production and   *1962*
Distribution of
Knowledge in the
United States

Fritz Machlup

*T*he Production and *Distribution of Knowledge in the United States* marked the beginning of the study of our post-industrial information society. Austrian-born economist Fritz Machlup had focused his research on the patent system, but he came to realize that patents were simply one part of a much bigger "knowledge economy." He then expanded the scope of his work to evaluate everything from stationery and typewriters to advertising to presidential addresses—anything that involved the activity of telling anyone anything. *The Production and Distribution of Knowledge in the United States* then revealed the new and startling shape of the U.S. economy.

Machlup's cool appraisal of the data showed that the knowledge industry accounted for nearly 29 percent of the U.S. gross national product, and that 43 percent of the civilian labor force consisted of knowledge transmitters or full-time knowledge receivers. Indeed, the proportion of the labor force involved in the knowledge economy increased from 11 to 32 percent between 1900 and 1959—a monumental shift.

Beyond documenting this revolution, Machlup founded the wholly new field of information economics. The transformation to a knowledge economy has resonated throughout the rest of the century, especially with the rise of the Internet. As two recent observers noted, "Information goods—from movies and music to software code and stock quotes—have supplanted industrial goods as the key drivers of world markets." Continued study of this change and its effects is testament to Fritz Machlup's pioneering work.

1963 *Linear Programming and Extensions*

George B. Dantzig

PRINCETON LANDMARKS
IN MATHEMATICS

George B. Dantzig

Linear Programming and Extensions

George Dantzig is properly acclaimed as the "father of linear programming." Linear programming is a mathematical technique used to optimize a situation. It can be used to minimize traffic congestion or to maximize the scheduling of airline flights. He formulated its basic theoretical model and discovered its underlying computational algorithm, the "simplex method," in a pathbreaking memorandum published by the United States Air Force in early 1948. *Linear Programming and Extensions* provides an extraordinary account of the subsequent development of his subject, including research in mathematical theory, computation, economic analysis, and applications to industrial problems.

Dantzig first achieved success as a statistics graduate student at the University of California, Berkeley. One day he arrived for a class after it had begun, and assumed the two problems on the board were assigned for homework. When he handed in the solutions, he apologized to his professor, Jerzy Neyman, for their being late but explained that he had found the problems harder than usual. About six weeks later, Neyman excitedly told Dantzig, "I've just written an introduction to one of your papers. Read it so I can send it out right away for publication." Dantzig had no idea what he was talking about. He later learned that the "homework" problems had in fact been two famous unsolved problems in statistics.

A Monetary History   1963
of the United States,
1867–1960

Milton Friedman and
Anna Jacobson
Schwartz

Writing in the June
1965 issue of the
Economic Journal, Harry
G. Johnson begins with a
sentence seemingly cali-
brated to the scale of the
book he set himself to review: "The long-awaited
monetary history of the United States by Friedman and Schwartz
is in every sense of the term a monumental scholarly achievement—monumental in its sheer bulk, monumental in the defini-
tiveness of its treatment of innumerable issues, large and small
. . . monumental, above all, in the theoretical and statistical effort
and ingenuity that have been brought to bear on the solution of
complex and subtle economic issues."

Friedman and Schwartz marshaled massive historical data and
sharp analytics to support the claim that monetary policy—steady
control of the money supply—matters profoundly in the management of the nation's economy, especially in navigating serious
economic fluctuations. In their influential chapter 7, "The Great
Contraction"—which Princeton published in 1965 as a separate
paperback—they address the central economic event of the century, the Depression. According to Hugh Rockoff, writing in January 2000: "If Great Depressions could be prevented through
timely actions by the monetary authority (or by a monetary rule),
as Friedman and Schwartz had contended, then the case for market economies was measurably stronger."

Milton Friedman won the Nobel Prize in Economics in 1976
for work related to *A Monetary History* as well as to his other
Princeton University Press book, *A Theory of the Consumption
Function* (1957).

Economics at the Center of the Mathematical Universe

Sylvia Nasar

"Small events at times can have large consequences," write Milton Friedman and Anna Schwartz in *A Monetary History of the United States* (1963), paraphrasing Shakespeare in *Richard III*. At one point, they trace the greatest economic calamity in the last century, the Great Depression, to the untimely death of a single individual. "Because no great strength would be required to hold back the rock that starts a landslide," they argue, "it does not follow that the landslide will not be of major proportions."

Friedman and Schwartz's study set off an intellectual avalanche that ultimately altered the landscape of economic thinking—just as the authors intended. So, in fact, did a half dozen or so other books published by Princeton in the 1940s, 1950s, and 1960s that have since attained the status of classics. That's an impressive record for a press that ignored economics entirely before World War II, dedicated just 1 percent of its titles to the topic for the next forty years, and acquired an actual economics *list* only in the last fifteen—all while MIT, Harvard, and McGraw-Hill dominated the market. As Paul Samuelson, sitting in his MIT office in Cambridge, Massachusetts, said the other day, "Princeton had the mathematicians; *we* had the economists."

But Princeton's tilt toward mathematics actually helps explain some of Princeton's biggest successes. A little history will show why: By the time World War II started, Princeton had become the world capital of mathematics. Intellectuals from Russia and from eastern and central Europe—including top mathematicians and physicists—had been flocking to the United States to escape revolution, war, economic collapse, and anti-Semitism since the 1920s. Princeton had opened its arms (and wallets) to the newcomers, going so far as to establish the Institute for Advanced Study, an Olympus comprising equal parts German university and Vienna café, to make them feel at home. Inside the Princeton town line, the belief that "the human mind could accomplish anything with mathematical ideas"—specifically, that mathematics could do for the social sciences what it had done for the natural ones—seemed no more far-fetched than expecting to bump into Albert Einstein or Kurt Gödel on Mercer Street.

By the end of the war, economists had adopted mathematics as their new lingua franca. As Roger Backhouse reports in his superb history of economics, *The Ordinary Business of Life* (Princeton, 2002), so many mathematically sophisticated émigrés went into economics that nearly half the contributors to the *American Economic Review* in 1945 were European-born. What's more, the war had given scores of young economists the opportunity to work shoulder-to-shoulder with mathematicians, physicists, engineers, and the like. Milton Friedman, who had been at the Department of Treasury during the New Deal, spent most of the war at the top secret Statistical Research Group at Columbia; Paul Samuelson's day job was at MIT's Radiation Lab; and Kenneth Arrow, who had joined the army, produced weather forecasts for the D-Day invasion.

The success of economists in advising the military on how to inflict maximum damage at minimum cost or, at the very least, how to move millions of men and cargoes by the cheapest route, convinced many of them of the applicability and effectiveness of mathematical methods. At least one, Wassily Leontief, used a computer to construct a giant economic model. Within a few years, some universities decided to allow Ph.D. candidates to substitute fluency in mathematics for a reading knowledge of French or German. One observer complained, circa 1952, "These days you can hardly tell a mathematical economist from an ordinary economist."

The point is that, having specialized in mathematics, Princeton had a comparative advantage when economists decided they wanted to use more math. Put another way, Princeton University Press didn't need a long list of economics titles to have a large impact—just enough of the right ones. *Theory of Games and Economic Behavior* (1944) is such a book. A reflection of the zeitgeist, the book was the product of a collaboration between a mathematician from Budapest and an economist from Vienna. John von Neumann practically invented the branch of mathematics called game theory, but a book about its potential uses in economics was Oskar Morgenstern's idea. According to historian Robert Leonard, who is working on an intellectual biography of von Neumann, Morgenstern knew about as much mathematics as von Neumann knew economics. But ignorance of the other's discipline was an incentive to collaborate. Ultimately, the coauthors were forced to do their readers the favor of spelling out their thoughts doubly, once in symbols, a second time in English.

Theory of Games is a pitch for using new mathematics to make economics more useful. The authors point to a gaping hole in existing theory—it can't handle situations where one outcome depends on another—and then outline a strategy for fixing it. Any economic outcome involving interdependence can be defined as the solution to a game between two or more players, they write, and therefore can be analyzed through game theory. Along the way, they develop the first coherent theory of how rational individuals choose among different options that are more or less likely.

One British reviewer couldn't decide whether *Theory of Games* was "a great classic" or a "mere complicated mathematical puzzle void of practical relevance." That was a fairly typical reaction, since it looked for a while as if the mathematics would scare away most economists and the economics would turn off most mathematicians. The authors' haughty disdain for existing economic theory didn't endear them to readers either. They, and the Press, were saved by a front-page *New York Times* story depicting game theory as a weapon in the Cold War.

Ironically, the book owes its publication less to editorial vision than to an anonymous donor. The war was in its third year, paper was costly, and the manuscript was "mammoth," having ballooned from a "pamphlet" of 100 or so pages into a doorstop of 1,200. The trustees of the Press balked, demanding that the university, or the Institute for Advanced Study, or some other donor contribute $3,000 (the equivalent of $32,000 today). Things looked bleak for a month or two, but finally a telegram reached von Neumann in Atlantic City in late September: "Delighted to inform you publication of your book assured." Relieved, he returned to Los Alamos, where he told Robert Oppenheimer, chief of the Manhattan Project, that he could now devote his spare time to the physics of implosion.

Paul Samuelson wasn't so lucky. In *The Foundations of Economic Analysis* (Harvard, 1947) Samuelson recast virtually the whole of economic theory in the precise language of mathematics and showed that many seemingly disparate situations could be treated as optimization problems. Samuelson submitted a first draft as his Ph.D. thesis in 1941 at age twenty-five and finished the entire manuscript while working on lasers in 1944. But *Foundations* didn't appear for another three years. What's more, when it finally was published, the chairman of Harvard's economics department insisted that Harvard University Press destroy the metal plates after the five hundredth copy had been printed. Cambridge may have had the economists, but Princeton had the advantage of being less hostile to their use of mathematics.

• • •

It must be said that Princeton failed to exploit its first-mover advantage—quite possibly because Princeton's pure mathematicians had no more appreciation of economics as a discipline than the Institute had for the MANIAC, von Neumann's mainframe computer. Still, there were some important exceptions. In 1962, with the information technology revolution still embryonic, the Press published the first-ever attempt to describe and measure the *information* economy, *The Production and Distribution of Knowledge* (1962) by Fritz Machlup. Machlup, who had worked with Morgenstern in Vienna, drew on the theories of Ludwig von Mises and Friedrich Hayek about how markets generate and employ information. George Dantzig's *Linear Programming* (1963) introduces a method for solving problems like one that Dantzig actually solved during the war: how to supply American GIs with the necessary vitamins and minerals during World War II at the lowest possible cost. In the book, Dantzig describes how he and his team spent a total of 130 man-days with desk calculators to solve a system of 9 equations and 27 unknowns. His method, inspired by Leontief's input-output model, has become standard for solving transportation, scheduling, and allocation problems involving hundreds of thousands of variables; it helped start a field dedicated to finding new ways to economize on computation time.

Princeton also published one of the first books to apply high-powered mathematics to finance, *Spectral Analysis* (1964) by Clive Granger. Last year, Granger won a Nobel for that work which has proved particularly valuable in forecasting economic variables. Interestingly, Oskar Morgenstern, who founded Mathematica—a consulting firm staffed by Princeton professors that used cutting-edge mathematical techniques—was present at the creation in this case as well. The pitfalls and drawbacks of commonly used methods for analyzing time series constituted another of Morgenstern's pet peeves. In the 1960s, he and Granger applied spectrum analysis—a technique for separating noise in the data from trends—to stock data.

• • •

No twentieth-century work of economic history has had the impact on economic *policy* of Friedman and Schwartz's monumental study. What on earth was Princeton doing, anyway, publishing one of the pillars of the so-called Chicago School? It was just part of a deal that Princeton had with the National Bureau of Economic Research, which sponsored the study. Arthur Burns, the legendary Fed chairman and head of the NBER in the 1950s, suggested that Friedman and Schwartz would make a perfect team despite the fact that one lived in Chicago, the other in New York. For half a dozen years they were. "Chapters went back and forth," recalled Anna Schwartz recently. "Statistical tables went back and forth. Of course there were disagreements."

The result had the heft and narrative sweep of a three-decker by Trollope, Schwartz's favorite author. It was also a wide-ranging attack, backed by a mass of minutely detailed statistics rather than fancy econometric techniques, on the prevailing Keynesian consensus. Instead of agreeing that markets were inherently unstable and that monetary policy was of little help in preventing depressions, the authors blamed the Great Depression on fatal errors by the Federal Reserve and tried to show that better monetary policy would have prevented the global slump. Not surprisingly, given that it was published the year that the Kennedy tax cut was proposed, the *Monetary History* was greeted with skepticism or else ignored. The Federal Reserve, which had supplied the data, maintained a dignified silence, but Chairman William McChesney Martin secretly commissioned a rival scholar to produce a rebuttal.

Just as the 1919 eclipse validated Einstein's theory of relativity, the failure of fiscal policies to end the 1970s stagflation eventually made the *Monetary History*—especially its chapter on the Great Depression—required reading. The effect on the profession is reflected in Samuelson's best-selling textbook, *Economics*. In the 1948 edition, as a study of successive editions notes, Samuelson maintains that "few economists regard Federal Reserve monetary policy as a panacea for controlling the business cycle." By 1985, Samuelson and coauthor William Nordhaus insist, "Money is the most powerful and useful tool that macroeconomic policymakers have."

• • •

When Princeton University Press finally decided to make economics a priority, it returned to its roots in mathematics. In the interval since 1944, econometrics—mathematical and statistical tools for testing economic hypotheses—had become standard equipment. In fact, the very first and the latest Nobel Prizes were given for contributions in econometrics. James Hamilton's *Time Series Analysis* (1994) is an important handbook for researchers trying to understand the uses and pitfalls of the enormous array of techniques developed for coping with the very problems that Clive Granger began to focus on in the early 1960s. Similarly, John Campbell, Andrew Lo, and Craig MacKinlay's *Econometrics of Financial Markets* (1997) is another highly regarded compendium of problems and techniques for researchers in finance, the area where the growth of mathematical applications has been most explosive. *Irrational Exuberance* (2000) by Robert Shiller, on the other hand, was aimed at investors, not researchers. Warning that the nineties' stock bubble was about to burst, the book landed on the *New York Times* best-seller list.

These days Princeton's list is especially strong in game theory. Modern corporations engage in life-and-death competition to make new products by new means, but they also cooperate by licensing proprietary knowledge to competitors. Von Neumann and Morgenstern offered no methods for analyzing such complex cases. By contrast, *A Course in Microeconomic Theory* (1990) by David Kreps, which reflects the contributions of John Nash, John Harsanyi, Reinhardt Selten, and many others since the 1940s, is a milestone marking the transition from an exotic novelty to the closest thing to a unified field theory of economics. It's somehow quite fitting that one of last year's additions to the now crowded economics list was the sixtieth anniversary edition of von Neumann and Morgenstern's *Theory of Games*.

A former economics correspondent for the New York Times, *Sylvia Nasar is the Knight Professor of Journalism at Columbia University. She is the author of the celebrated biography* A Beautiful Mind: The Life of Mathematical Genius and Nobel Laureate John Nash *and coeditor of Princeton's* The Essential John Nash *(2001).*

Morse Theory 1963

J. Milnor

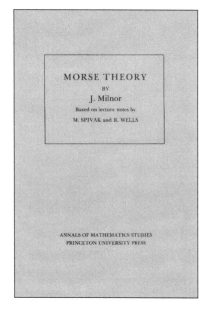

One of the most cited books in mathematics, John Milnor's exposition of Morse theory has been the most important book on the subject for more than forty years. Morse theory was developed in the 1920s by mathematician Marston Morse. (Morse was on the faculty of the Institute for Advanced Study, and Princeton published his *Topological Methods in the Theory of Functions of a Complex Variable* in the Annals of Mathematics Studies series in 1947.) One classical application of Morse theory includes the attempt to understand, with only limited information, the large-scale structure of an object. This kind of problem occurs in mathematical physics, dynamic systems, and mechanical engineering. Morse theory has received much attention in the last two decades as a result of a famous paper in which theoretical physicist Edward Witten relates Morse theory to quantum field theory.

Milnor was awarded the Fields Medal (the mathematical equivalent of a Nobel Prize) in 1962 for his work in differential topology. He has since received the National Medal of Science (1967) and the Steele Prize from the American Mathematical Society twice (1982 and 2004) in recognition of his explanations of mathematical concepts across a wide range of scientific disciplines. The citation reads, "The phrase sublime elegance is rarely associated with mathematical exposition, but it applies to all of Milnor's writings. Reading his books, one is struck with the ease with which the subject is unfolding and it only becomes apparent after reflection that this ease is the mark of a master."

Milnor has published five books with Princeton University Press.

1963 *The Civic Culture:*
Political Attitudes
and Democracy in
Five Nations

Gabriel A. Almond
and Sidney Verba

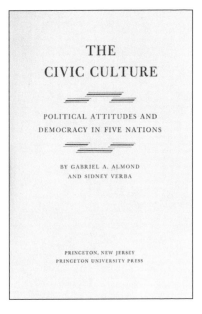

THE
CIVIC CULTURE

POLITICAL ATTITUDES AND
DEMOCRACY IN FIVE NATIONS

BY GABRIEL A. ALMOND
AND SIDNEY VERBA

PRINCETON, NEW JERSEY
PRINCETON UNIVERSITY PRESS

What attitudes sustain successful democracy? How can its features be replicated? Using surveys and interviews conducted in Britain and the United States (as examples of successful democracies) and Germany, Mexico, and Italy (as examples of developing democracies), Gabriel Almond and Sidney Verba attempted to answer these questions and, by doing so, to get to the heart of democratic political culture. They argued that the most distinctive characteristic of political life in the twentieth century was the newfound political power of the ordinary citizen.

The Civic Culture represented the best early fruit of a new research agenda in political science—focusing on the attitudes and behavior of ordinary citizens. Following its lead, political scientists began to replace their previous inclination to conduct largely legal studies of formal political institutions with a concern for how individuals related to the political system in formal and informal ways. Seminal books like *The Civic Culture* spawned a generation of comparative research that changed the way political scientists studied politics at home and abroad. It continues to influence work on civic engagement and democratization. Robert Putnam, the author of *Bowling Alone*, has said of *The Civic Culture*, "Few books in political science of the last three or four decades have had the impact and continuing power of *The Civic Culture.*" The late Aaron Wildavsky said, "*The Civic Culture* remains the best study of comparative political culture in our time."

SPECTRAL ANALYSIS
OF ECONOMIC TIME
SERIES

BY C. W. J. GRANGER
IN ASSOCIATION WITH
M. HATANAKA

1964
PRINCETON UNIVERSITY PRESS
PRINCETON, NEW JERSEY

Spectral Analysis of Economic Time Series   1964

C.W.J. Granger, in association with M. Hatanaka

In *Spectral Analysis of Economic Time Series*, Clive Granger showed that then-established statistical methods were inadequate to the analysis of economic variables such as stock prices, interest rates, and GDP, which tend to drift over long periods without reverting to a stationary point. Drawing upon work done by members of the Time Series Project of the Econometric Research Program of Princeton University, Granger developed spectral analysis, a technique for inspecting such cyclical phenomena, and introduced it into the study of time series (chronological observations of changes in economic variables). This technique helped economists address the problem of feedback between economic variables and allowed for more realistic and accurate accounting by economists of time series data.

Granger's volume would help establish the econometric foundations of modern economics. Michio Hatanaka's two chapters, which conclude the book, discuss applications of cross-spectral analysis to business cycles and inventory cycles.

Nearly four decades after the publication of *Spectral Analysis of Economic Time Series*, Granger won the 2003 Nobel Prize for Economics. The Nobel Foundation noted that the methods developed by Granger had become invaluable in areas of economic research and policy including "the relations between wealth and consumption, exchange rates and price levels, and short- and long-term interest rates."

1965 *Princeton*
Encyclopedia
of Poetry
and Poetics

Edited by Alex
Preminger

I consider this volume nearly as
essential for any working poet
as a good dictionary.

—*Judson Jerome,* Writer's
Digest

PRINCETON
ENCYCLOPEDIA
OF POETRY
AND POETICS

ALEX PREMINGER
EDITOR

FRANK J. WARNKE AND O. B. HARDISON, JR.
ASSOCIATE EDITORS

Enlarged Edition

PRINCETON, NEW JERSEY
PRINCETON UNIVERSITY PRESS

From "abecedarius" (an acrostic poem) to "zeugma" (yoking unlike words), the *Princeton Encyclopedia of Poetry and Poetics* is a reference gold mine that resulted from the cumulative efforts of a distinguished group of literary scholars and writers, spearheaded by its devoted editor Alex Preminger, an assistant librarian at Princeton University. This one-of-a-kind reference work was his life's work. First published in 1965, the original version quickly became a treasure-filled reference for students and scholars of poetry and literature in general. Among the 215 original contributors were Northrop Frye writing on allegory, Murray Krieger on belief in poetry, Philip Wheelwright on myth, John Hollander on music, and William Carlos Williams on free verse.

In 1974, the Enlarged Edition multiplied the entries with dozens of new subjects, including rock 'n' roll lyrics, computer poetry, and black poetry, to name just a few. In its most recent incarnation, published in 1993, the "new" *Encyclopedia*, fully revised by T.V.F. Brogan, expanded the contents of the reference work even further to incorporate the explosion of theoretical and methodological interests in the field during the 1970s and 1980s. Along with extensive revisions to previous entries, this edition included new topics such as cultural criticism, discourse, feminist poetics, and Chicano poetry. Contributing for the first time were Elaine Showalter on feminist poetics, Houston Baker on the Harlem Renaissance, and Andrew Ross on Marxist criticism—among others.

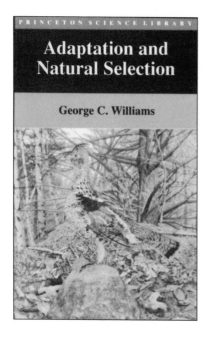

Adaptation and Natural Selection: A Critique of Some Current Evolutionary Thought   **1966**

George C. Williams

*A*daptation and Natural Selection began as a polemic. In the 1930s, the evolutionary biologists Ronald A. Fisher, J.B.S. Haldane, and Sewall Wright had combined Darwinian natural selection with Mendelian genetics to develop a rigorous mathematical evolutionary theory. But thirty years after this "modern synthesis," George Williams found that evolutionary thought had grown flabby and popular understanding woefully inaccurate.

In 1966, simple Darwinism, which holds that evolution functions primarily at the level of the individual organism, was threatened by opposing concepts such as group selection, a popular idea that evolution acts to select entire species rather than individuals. In this book, Williams famously argued in favor of the Darwinists and struck a powerful blow against those in opposing camps.

In particular, he proposed that in studying adaptation, biologists should focus on the simplest form of natural selection—alternative alleles in Mendelian populations. He also urged biologists to treat adaptation as a special and onerous concept that should be used only where absolutely necessary. It was not adaptation that led the flying fish to fall back into the water; it was gravity.

With others, Williams helped restore Darwinian evolution as a blind process driven by genetic variation and selection. The book remains a remarkably crisp introduction to what evolution is and what it is not.

1967 The Theory of
Island Biogeography

Robert H. MacArthur
and Edward O. Wilson

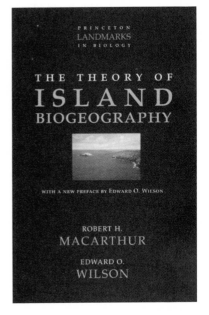

The young biologists Robert MacArthur and Ed Wilson argued that in 1967 ecology was stuck in a "natural history phase" dominated by the collection of data. In *The Theory of Island Biogeography* they set out to change that by developing a general mathematical theory that would make sense of a key ecological problem—island biogeography. MacArthur and Wilson built on first principles of population ecology and genetics to explain how distance and area combine to regulate the balance between immigration and extinction in island populations. Species diversity was not just a product of chance or historical events, the authors argued. It could in fact be analyzed by science.

The Theory of Island Biogeography transformed the science of biogeography. The equilibrium model outlined in the book has been at the center of that field since the book's publication. More fundamentally, the book transformed ecology. MacArthur and Wilson were both enthusiastic naturalists, but MacArthur was also gifted mathematically. The authors proposed that ecologists should use mathematics to simplify the natural world and gain analytical insight. By substituting even "a first, crude theory" for a large pile of facts, MacArthur and Wilson argued that ecology could begin to develop some general principles.

MacArthur and Wilson's compact book was also the first volume in the Monographs in Population Biology series. These inconspicuous yellow-spined titles quickly became the most important book series in ecology. Driven by the same impulses as *Theory of Island Biogeography*, the books brought theory and mathematics to bear on ecological data and led a discipline along with them.

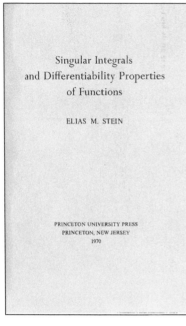

Singular Integrals
and Differentiability Properties
of Functions

ELIAS M. STEIN

PRINCETON UNIVERSITY PRESS
PRINCETON, NEW JERSEY
1970

Singular Integrals and Differentiability Properties of Functions

1970

Elias M. Stein

Singular integrals are among the most interesting and important objects of study in analysis, one of the three main branches of mathematics. They deal with real and complex numbers and their functions. In this book, Princeton professor Elias Stein, a leading mathematical innovator as well as a gifted expositor, produced what has been called the most influential mathematics text in the last thirty-five years. One reason for its success as a text is its almost legendary presentation: Stein takes arcane material, previously understood only by specialists, and makes it accessible even to beginning graduate students. Readers have reflected that when you read this book, not only do you see that the greats of the past have done exciting work, but you also feel inspired that you can master the subject and contribute to it yourself.

Singular integrals were known to only a few specialists when Stein's book was first published. Over time, however, the book has inspired a whole generation of researchers to apply its methods to a broad range of problems in many disciplines, including engineering, biology, and finance.

Stein has received numerous awards for his research, including the Wolf Prize of Israel, the Steele Prize, and the National Medal of Science. He has published eight books with Princeton, including *Real Analysis* in 2005.

1970 On the Medieval Origins of the Modern State

Joseph R. Strayer

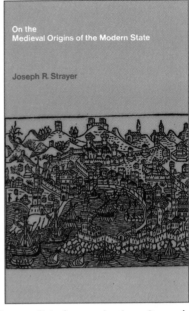

On the
Medieval Origins of the Modern State

Joseph R. Strayer

Today we take the state for granted. It dominates global political structures, and we can scarcely envisage life without it. But how did it come about? In *On the Medieval Origins of the Modern State*, historian Joseph Strayer demonstrated the relevance of medieval historical institutions to modern political organization. Strayer's brief and influential essay provided the key to understanding how and why the form of the European nation-state evolved.

For Strayer, the state enabled a more concentrated use of human resources than ever before; thus it is crucial to understand just how and why people's loyalty shifted from family, local community, or religious organization to the state and its institutions. Concentrating mainly on France and England, Strayer argues that the medieval rulers provided the foundation for the administrative and judicial practices of subsequent European monarchies. He points to jury trials, representative assemblies, and bureaucracies as examples of contemporary institutions with medieval roots and shows how medieval state builders had to invent and perfect instruments of justice and administration, create a cadre of loyal and efficient bureaucrats, and, most important, merit the allegiance that they demanded from their subjects.

On the Medieval Origins of the Modern State has become a classic of medieval and early modern European political history and a standard text in the field.

Marxism and Form: 1971
Twentieth-Century
Dialectical Theories
of Literature

Fredric Jameson

For more than thirty years, Fredric Jameson has been one of the most productive, wide-ranging, and distinctive literary theorists in the United States and the Anglophone world. *Marxism and Form* provided a pioneering account of the work of the major European Marxist theorists—T. W. Adorno, Walter Benjamin, Herbert Marcuse, Ernst Bloch, Georg Lukács, and Jean-Paul Sartre—work that was, at the time, largely neglected in the English-speaking world. Through penetrating readings of each theorist, Jameson developed a critical mode of engagement that has had tremendous influence. He provided a framework for analyzing the connection between art and the historical circumstances of its making—in particular, how cultural artifacts distort, repress, or transform their circumstances through the abstractions of aesthetic form.

Jameson's presentation of the critical thought of this Hegelian Marxism provided a stark alternative to the Anglo-American tradition of empiricism and humanism. It would later provide a compelling alternative to poststructuralism and deconstruction as they became dominant methodologies in aesthetic criticism.

One year after *Marxism and Form*, Princeton published Jameson's *The Prison-House of Language* (1972), which provided a thorough historical and philosophical description of formalism and structuralism. Both books remain central to Jameson's main intellectual legacy: describing and extending a tradition of Western Marxism in cultural theory and literary interpretation.

1973 *Stability and Complexity in Model Ecosystems*

Robert M. May

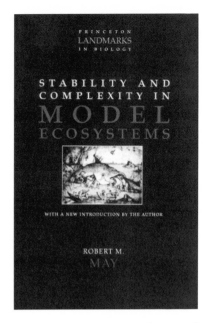

What makes populations stabilize? What makes them fluctuate? Are populations in complex ecosystems more stable than populations in simple ecosystems? In 1973, Robert May addressed these questions in this monograph that has since become a classic. Trained as a theoretical physicist, May used mathematical modeling to investigate the stability and complexity of a community of interacting plants and animals, following the food web as a clue. Contrary to general biological thinking, he showed in population dynamics models that population equilibrium was less likely to destabilize such ecosystems when the number of species is increased and species interactions are randomly added.

In the quarter century since its publication, the book's message has grown in power. *Stability and Complexity in Model Ecosystems* played a key role in introducing nonlinear mathematical models, along with the study of deterministic chaos, to ecologists—as science writer James Gleick would chronicle in his best-seller *Chaos*. Nonlinear models are now at the center of ecological thinking, and current threats to biodiversity have made questions about the role of ecosystem complexity more crucial than ever. This book launched a career of mathematical insight into some of life's biggest questions.

Robert May has gone on to apply mathematical modeling to other biological problems. He has modeled the current state of biodiversity and extinction patterns, arguing for the necessity of responding immediately to this crisis. He has also developed mathematical models of infectious disease that are now used by governments and NGOs to tackle diseases like AIDS.

Stable and Random   **1973**
Motions in Dynam-
ical Systems: With
Special Emphasis on
Celestial Mechanics

Jürgen Moser

One of the world's lead-
ing mathematicians,
Jürgen Moser developed
theories in celestial me-
chanics and many other
aspects of mathematics.
He is most renowned for
his work on the Kolmogorov-Arnold-Moser theorem.

Stable and Random Motions in Dynamical Systems examines
how to decide when a dynamical system has stable or unstable behavior. The book was motivated by the stability problem in celestial mechanics: can we prove that the solar system is stable? Moser
explains the historical roots of the question, makes it precise, and
sets up the mathematical questions that the rest of the book
addresses: the Kolmogorov-Arnold-Moser theorem, dealing with
quasi-periodic motions, and the Smale-Birkhoff theorem, con-
necting dynamical systems with Bernoulli processes. These are
the "stable" and "random" aspects to which the title alludes. The
book resulted from the inaugural Hermann Weyl Lectures at the
Institute for Advanced Study in 1972.

Originally published in the Annals of Mathematics Studies series, the book was reissued in the Princeton Landmarks in Mathematics series in 2001. In the foreword to this most recent edition,
Princeton mathematician Philip J. Holmes wrote, "After almost
thirty years, Moser's lectures are still one of the best entrées to the
fascinating worlds of order and chaos in dynamics."

Sabbatai Sevi:
The Mystical
Messiah, 1626–1676

Gershom Gerhard
Scholem

Translated from the German

BOLLINGEN XCIII

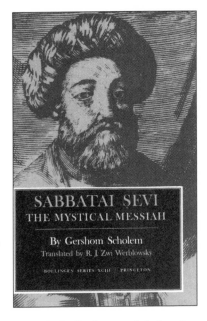

The twentieth century
produced a galaxy of
extraordinary Jewish his-
torians. Gershom Scholem
stands out among them
for the richness and power
of his historical imagination. Born in Berlin in 1897, Scholem became a Zionist as a young student in a revolt against his family's
bourgeois and assimilated life. He learned Hebrew and studied
Kabbalah, the world of mystical teachings that had become mar-
ginalized—indeed stigmatized—within the mainstream rationalist Jewish tradition. In 1923, Scholem emigrated to Palestine and
eventually joined the faculty of the Hebrew University of Jerusalem, publishing groundbreaking studies in the field of Jewish
mysticism.

In the 1930s, Scholem's scholarship turned to an obscure kab-
balist rabbi of seventeenth-century Turkey, Sabbatai Sevi, who
aroused a fervent following that spread over the Jewish world
after he declared himself to be the Messiah. The movement suffered a severe blow when Sevi was forced to convert to Islam, but
a clandestine sect survived. A Bollingen Foundation grant enabled Scholem to complete the original Hebrew edition of his biography in 1957. Bollingen also supported R. J. Zwi Werblowsky's
masterful English translation. A monumental and revisionary
work of Jewish historiography, *Sabbatai Sevi* stands out for its
combination of philological and empirical authority and for its
passion. It is widely esteemed as one of Scholem's masterworks.
The author himself always regarded the Princeton/Bollingen edition as a highlight of his scholarship.

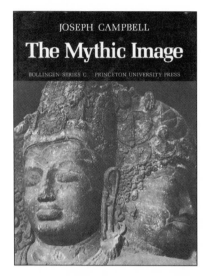

JOSEPH CAMPBELL

The Mythic Image

BOLLINGEN SERIES C.   PRINCETON UNIVERSITY PRESS

The Mythic Image   1974

Joseph Campbell

BOLLINGEN C

Mythologist Joseph Campbell was a masterful storyteller, able to weave tales from every corner of the world into compelling, even spellbinding, narratives. His interest in comparative mythology began in childhood, when the young Joe Campbell was taken to see Buffalo Bill's Wild West Show at Madison Square Garden. He started writing articles on Native American mythology in high school, and the parallels between age-old myths and the mythic themes in literature and dreams became a lifelong preoccupation. Campbell's best-known work is *The Hero with a Thousand Faces* (1949), which became a *New York Times* paperback best-seller for Princeton in 1988 after Campbell's star turn on the Bill Moyers television program *The Power of Myth*.

During his early years as a professor of comparative religion at Sarah Lawrence College, Campbell made the acquaintance of Indologist Heinrich Zimmer, a kindred spirit who introduced him to Paul and Mary Mellon, the founders of Bollingen Series. They chose Campbell's *Mythic Image* as the culmination of the series, giving it the closing position—number one hundred. A lavishly illustrated and beautifully produced study of the mythology of the world's high civilizations, *The Mythic Image* received a front-cover review in the *New York Times Book Review* upon publication. Through the medium of visual art, the book explores the relation of dreams to myth and demonstrates the important differences between oriental and occidental interpretations of dreams and life.

1974　*The Freud/Jung Letters: The Correspondence between Sigmund Freud and C. G. Jung*

Edited by William McGuire

BOLLINGEN SERIES XCIV

I am confident that you will often be in a position to back me up, but I shall also gladly accept correction." So wrote Freud in his first letter to Jung in 1906. Over the next eight years the tenor and tone of their correspondence changed dramatically, reflecting the growing differences in their approach to the theory and practice of psychology and psychoanalysis. Their disagreements, captured here, led to the dissolution of their relationship as mentor and student. Jung's break with Freud is one of the most famous stories in the early history of psychoanalytic thought. As late as 1959 Jung was moved to refer to the letters as "that accursed correspondence."

The eventual publication of the Freud/Jung letters was a testament to the diplomacy and persistence of William McGuire, executive editor for Bollingen Series. He managed to secure the agreement of both the Freud and the Jung trustees in the face of what seemed insurmountable difficulties. The book generated a frenzy of media interest by providing unparalleled insights into the love/hate relationship between two of the century's most influential intellectual protagonists. As Lionel Trilling wrote in the *New York Times Book Review*, "Both as it bears upon the personal lives of the men between whom the letters passed and upon the intellectual history of our epoch, it is a document of inestimable importance."

Bollingen Series, 1943–2002

Bollingen Series, named for the small village in Switzerland where Carl Gustav Jung had a private retreat, was originated by the philanthropist Paul Mellon and his first wife, Mary Conover Mellon, in 1943. Both Mellons were analysands of Jung in Switzerland in the 1930s and had been welcomed into his personal circle, which included the eclectic group of scholars who had recently inaugurated the prestigious conferences known as the Eranos Lectures, held annually in Ascona, Switzerland.

In 1945 the couple established Bollingen Foundation as a source of fellowships and subventions related to humanistic scholarship and institutions, but its grounding mission came to be the Bollingen book series. The original inspiration for the series had been Mary Mellon's wish to publish a comprehensive English-language translation of the works of Jung. In Paul Mellon's words, "The idea of the *Collected Works of Jung* might be considered the central core, the binding factor, not only of the Foundation's general direction but also of the intellectual temper of Bollingen Series as a whole."

In his famous Bollingen Tower, Jung pursued studies in the religions and cultures of the world (both ancient and modern), symbolism, mysticism, the occult (especially alchemy), and, of course, psychology. The breadth of Jung's interests allowed the Bollingen editors to attract scholars, artists, and poets from among the brightest lights in midcentury Europe and America, whether or not their work was "Jungian" in orientation. In the end, the series was remarkably eclectic and wide-ranging, with fewer than half of its titles written by Jung or his followers.

Mary Mellon was the first editor of the series, and Helen and Kurt Wolff, founders of Pantheon Books in New York, were its publishers. Conceived as a closed series of 100 numbered projects, some multivolume, the series would end up with more than 275 books bearing its imprint. After Mary Mellon's untimely death in 1946, her husband continued to support the series and the foundation in her memory. Jack Barnett succeeded Mary as the series' editor, remaining with the imprint for nearly twenty years. The series came to Princeton after the Wolffs retired in 1961 and sold Pantheon Books to Random House. Paul Mellon then sought a university press that would take over not only production and distribution functions from Pantheon but the entirety of the foundation's editorial and administrative duties. He chose Princeton

University Press for this task, and in 1967 the continuing enterprise of Bollingen Foundation came to Princeton.

Bollingen Series is so rich and so varied that the word "treasure trove" is not far-fetched, and a short summary cannot easily do it justice. What follows is a broad sampling of the range of titles contained in the series, though many more remain unmentioned. Especially significant books published after 1967 appear in the main text of this volume (see pp. 82, 83, 84, 126).

The first book in the series was one of a kind: Maud Oakes's *Where the Two Came to Their Father: A Navaho War Ceremonial* (1949), a meticulous documentation of Navaho shaman Jeff King's initiation ceremony, performed in 1943 to prepare young Navaho men who had just been drafted into the U.S. Army. Its original folio edition comprised a buckram folder of silk-screen prints of Oakes's reproductions of King's sand paintings, and an accompanying book with King's text and Joseph Campbell's interpretations. Legend has it that a silk-screen shop in Brooklyn closed its doors to all other work for six months in order to reproduce these beautiful images. The lavish production and award-winning book design exemplified by this first project were to become hallmarks of Bollingen Series.

The heart of the series, The Collected Works of C. G. Jung (XX) was published in twenty-one volumes between 1953 and 1979, with some additional appendix volumes published later. This brought together almost all of Jung's published writings, grouped by theme rather than by chronology; many of the texts appeared in new translations commissioned by Bollingen from R.F.C. Hull. Published in cooperation with Routledge and Kegan Paul in the UK, this massive undertaking was coordinated by William McGuire, first at the Bollingen offices in New York and finally at the Princeton offices. McGuire also edited the famous *Freud/Jung Letters* (XCIV) (see p. 84), and presided over the publication of the first three volumes in the later series collection, C. G. Jung Seminars (XCIX). McGuire's *Bollingen: An Adventure in Collecting the Past* (1982) is a fascinating history of all the people and projects involved in Bollingen Series and Bollingen Foundation fellowships; it carries a special Bollingen imprint even though it is not one of the numbered series titles.

Bollingen's greatest success, at least in terms of copies sold, belongs to the mythology and religion titles. The translation of a little-known Confucian classic *The I Ching, or Book of Changes*, with an introduction by Jung—originally published in two volumes in 1950 and reissued as a one-volume edition in 1964—

became a centerpiece of "New Age" culture in the 1960s and 1970s. More than a million copies of the one-volume edition have been sold. Echoing the enormous success of the *I Ching*, Joseph Campbell's *Hero with a Thousand Faces* (XVII), originally published in 1949, became a surprise *New York Times* paperback best-seller in 1988 when Bill Moyers broadcast a series of interviews with Campbell just months before his death, under the title *The Power of Myth*. (For more on Campbell, see p. 83) The series had published seminal works by most of the founding mothers and fathers of the New Age, including Mircea Eliade, whose *The Myth of the Eternal Return* (XLVI, 1954), *Yoga: Immortality and Freedom* (LVI, 1958), and *Shamanism: Archaic Techniques of Ecstasy* (LXXVI, 1964) continue to have a profound relevance for comparative religion. Erich Neumann's *The Great Mother* (XLVII, 1955) and *The Origins and History of Consciousness* (XLII, 1954), and Heinrich Zimmer's posthumously published *Myths and Symbols of Indian Art and Civilization* (VI, 1946), *Philosophies of India* (XXVI, 1951), and *The King and the Corpse* (XI, 1948), all edited by Joseph Campbell, remain foundational works. Other important works in mythology include Jung and Kerényi's *Essays on a Science of Mythology* (XXII, 1949), and J. J. Bachofen's classic nineteenth-century work translated for the first time into English, *Myth, Religion, and Mother Right* (LXXXIV, 1967). The counterculture's embrace of mythology, mysticism, and comparative religion was unforeseen by the editors, authors, and translators of these Bollingen books, who, with the exception of Joseph Campbell, were bemused by, if not hostile to, the sudden surge in popularity (and the inevitable trivialization) of their work.

Although for some the association with New Age culture would tarnish the luster of certain of these Bollingen classics, the contributions of these distinguished religious studies volumes are undeniable. D. T. Suzuki's magisterial *Zen and Japanese Culture* (LXIV, 1959) is his most influential study of Asian religion. On Islamic mysticism, Henri Corbin's *Creative Imagination in the Sūfism of Ibn 'Arabī* (XCI:1, 1969), now entitled *Alone with the Alone,* and *Spiritual Body and Celestial Earth* (XCI:2, 1977) and Louis Massignon's *The Passion of Al-Hallāj* in four volumes (XCVIII, 1982) were groundbreaking texts. Original works in history include *Ibn Khaldûn: The Muqaddimah* (1958 and 1967) in three volumes, later issued in a single-volume abridged edition; this fourteenth-century classic was the first Islamic attempt to catalog all of world history and remains a standard reference in historiography. The Bollingen edition, the only English translation of this very influential book, may be taken as the epitome of what Bollingen series was able to accomplish. In Native American religion, Gladys A. Reichard's *Navaho Religion* (XVIII, 1950) was a landmark in the field. Like many other Bollingen authors, the great historian of Jewish mysticism Gershom Scholem had been introduced to Bollingen's circle at the Eranos conferences, and Joseph Campbell's six volumes of edited Eranos papers (XXX, 1954–1968) remain a unique record of the creative genius of this group of scholars. (For more on Scholem, see p. 82.)

Bollingen supported many large-scale projects. In addition to the collected Jung, Bollingen published seven volumes of the *Selected Works of Miguel de Unamuno* (LXXXV), which was awarded a National Book Award for Anthony Kerrigan's translation; five volumes of Karl Kerényi's *Archetypal Images in Greek Religion* (LXV), translated by Ralph Manheim; and Erwin R. Goodenough's *Jewish Symbols in the Greco-Roman Period* (XXXVII), in thirteen volumes—a classic in Jewish studies for which Jacob Neusner provided a one-volume epitome in 1989. Perhaps the most elaborately produced number in the series was the six-volume *Egyptian Religious Texts and Representations* (XL), edited by Alexandre Piankoff, in collaboration with Natacha Rambova: this work included foldout drawings of Egyptian tomb paintings opening to as long as ten feet, and it occasioned the first translation into English of the *Egyptian Book of the Dead*. Bollingen also undertook a planned fourteen-volume project from one of the major centers of Greek mystery religions, *Samothrace* (LX, 1958–1998), unfinished in eleven volumes when the series closed in 2002. Among the largest undertakings, the two Coleridge series begun by Kathleen Coburn in the 1940s—the *Notebooks of Samuel Taylor Coleridge*, in four volumes of two books each; and *The Collected Works of Samuel Taylor Coleridge*, in sixteen volumes—marked the formal end of the series, with the publication of Coleridge's *Opus Maximum* in 2002.

The series made many ambitious contributions translating literary works into English. It published fifteen volumes of the *Collected Works of Paul Valéry* (XLV), edited by Jackson Mathews; the six volumes of Charles S. Singleton's translation and commentary on Dante's *Divine Comedy* (LXXX: *Inferno*, 1970; *Purgatorio*, 1973; and *Paradiso*, 1975); an unusual edition of George Chapman's seventeenth-century translations of the *Iliad* and the *Odyssey* (*Chapman's Homer*, XLI, 1957); three volumes of new translations of the poems, prose, plays, and libretti of Hofmannsthal, introduced by T. S. Eliot and Michael Hamburg, in *Hugo von Hof-*

mannsthal: Selected Writings (XXXIII); and André Malraux's *The Psychology of Art* (XXIV, 1950), which was later issued in an abridged edition as *The Voices of Silence* (1978). Bollingen also produced new editions of the Greek classics: a single-volume *Collected Dialogues of Plato*, edited by Edith Hamilton (LXXI, 1961), and a two-volume *Complete Works of Aristotle*, edited by Jonathan Barnes (1984).

A stormy episode in Bollingen's venture into literary translation stemmed from the publication of Vladimir Nabokov's controversial translation of Pushkin's *Eugene Onegin* (LXXII, 1964) in a four-volume set that included the text of the translated epic, Nabokov's commentary, and a facsimile of the original Russian edition. Nabokov's unadorned literal translation was panned in the *New York Review of Books* by his erstwhile best friend, Edmund Wilson, which led to a ferocious feud waged in a series of public letters that ended their long-standing relationship.

In 1949, in partnership with the National Gallery of Art, Bollingen Foundation established the annual A. W. Mellon Lectures in the Fine Arts (XXXV). This is the only part of Bollingen Series that continues to produce new volumes. Inaugurated by Jacques Maritain's *Creative Intuition in Art and Poetry* (1953), these publications highlight the work of an impressive array of the century's most significant art historians and critics. Chief among the Mellon Lectures books is Kenneth Clark's *The Nude: A Study in Ideal Form* (1956), a classic in art history. Perhaps the most influential of the Mellon Lectures books is E. H. Gombrich's *Art and Illusion: A Study in the Psychology of Pictorial Representation* (1960), the revolutionary treatment of perception and art. Other notable lecturers in the series included Jacques Barzun, Isaiah Berlin, Jacob Bronowski, Arthur Danto, Jaroslav Pelikan, Nikolaus Pevsner, Vincent Scully, Stephen Spender, Leo Steinberg, and Richard Wollheim (see p. 126).

Bollingen Series stands out in the landscape of twentieth-century publishing for its boldness, its range, and the distinguished author list. One could easily argue that it has not been equaled and will never be duplicated.

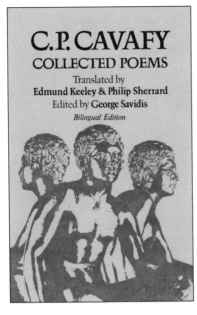

C. P. Cavafy:
Collected Poems

1975

Translated from
the Greek by
Edmund Keeley and
Philip Sherrard

The ancient city of Alexandria, Egypt, gave rise to one of the great modern poets, C. P. Cavafy (1863–1933). Generally recognized as the most original and influential Greek poet of the twentieth century, Cavafy lived not in Greece but in Alexandria, and briefly in London and Constantinople. His poetic talent flourished especially in the dynamic Mediterranean culture of Alexandria, and, in many poems, he gave a direct and personal voice to its homosexual subculture. His exceptional mythmaking powers have carried his reputation into the twenty-first century.

Included in Princeton's Modern Greek Studies series, the Keeley/Sherrard translation represents Cavafy's "canon" of 174 poems, plus 21 poems unpublished during his lifetime. James Merrill, writing in the *New York Review of Books*, praised this volume as "the best [English version] we are likely to see for some time." Thirty years later, it remains the standard translation.

The poem "Ithaka" came to national prominence in 1994. Jacqueline Kennedy Onassis counted it among her favorites and requested that it be read at her funeral. The *New York Times* reprinted the poem, which led to new printings and a spate of new Cavafy translations.

From "Ithaka"

Keep Ithaka always in your mind.
Arriving there is what you're destined for.
But don't hurry the journey at all.
Better if it lasts for years,

so you're old by the time you reach the island,
wealthy with all you've gained on the way,
not expecting Ithaka to make you rich.

Ithaka gave you the marvelous journey.
Without her you wouldn't have set out.
She has nothing left to give you now.

And if you find her poor, Ithaka won't have fooled you.
Wise as you will have become, so full of experience,
you'll have understood by then what these Ithakas mean.

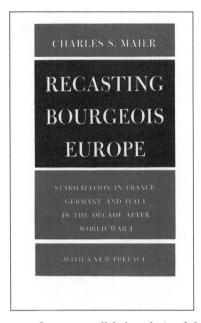

Recasting Bourgeois   **1975**
*Europe: Stabilization
in France, Germany,
and Italy in the
Decade after
World War I*

Charles S. Maier

The author of fourteen books, Charles Maier is one of the most prominent contemporary scholars of European history. *Recasting Bourgeois Europe*, his first book, presented an unparalleled analysis of the crucial decade in Europe after 1918. Based on extensive archival research in each of the three countries, the book examined how European societies progressed from a moment of social vulnerability to one of political and economic stabilization.

Recasting Bourgeois Europe accomplished two major historiographical goals simultaneously. First, Maier provided a comparative history of three different European societies for a period when common developments demanded an approach other than that of the usual national histories. Second, he rethought the political structure of the European interwar period. Although most accounts presented the 1920s as a time characterized by illusory attempts to return to a prewar political equilibrium, and doomed to succumb to the Depression and the dictatorships, Maier suggested instead that the stabilization of the 1920s, vulnerable as it was, foreshadowed the more enduring political stability achieved after World War II.

The immense and ambitious scope of this book, its ability to follow diverse but unified histories in detail, and its effort to make stabilization, and not just breakdown, a historical problem have made it a classic of European historiography.

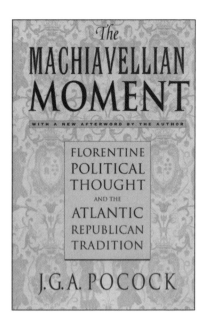

1975 *The Machiavellian*
Moment: Florentine
Political Thought
and the Atlantic
Republican Tradition

J.G.A. Pocock

This undisputed modern classic defies conventional categorization. The book's range is so wide and the number of debates it sparked in different disciplines so numerous that, as Philip Pettit has written, it "gave historians and philosophers a generation's work." But some things are certain: *The Machiavellian Moment* has become an authoritative source for our understanding of the republican tradition and, in particular, its adversarial relationship to liberalism.

Pocock showed that, as Machiavelli sought to revive classical republican ideals, his prime concern was the moment when a new republic first confronts the problem of maintaining the stability of its ideals and institutions—the "Machiavellian moment" of the book's title. After examining this problem in its sixteenth-century Italian context, Pocock took the bold and unexpected step of leaping forward to eighteenth-century America. He examined the anxieties of early American statesmen and citizens as they witnessed commercial expansion and feared for the imminent demise of their republic, and, in this Machiavellian moment, Pocock identified a language of civic virtue and civic humanism. The book has come to represent the so-called republican synthesis, which holds that America was born with a fear of corruption and a desire to promote classical virtue.

Soon after publication, Pocock's arguments spawned furious debate among intellectual historians that spread to political philosophy and American history in general. Over time, *The Machiavellian Moment* has become a must-read book for anyone who wants to understand the intellectual origins of Western politics.

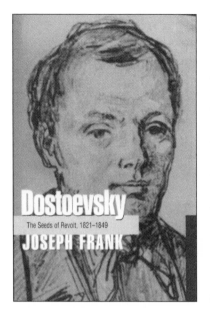

Dostoevsky: The Seeds of Revolt, 1821–1849

Also: *Dostoevsky: The Years of Ordeal, 1850–1859* [1983]

Dostoevsky: The Stir of Liberation, 1860–1865 [1986]

Dostoevsky: The Miraculous Years, 1865–1871 [1995]

Dostoevsky: The Mantle of the Prophet, 1871–1881 [2000]

Joseph Frank

The term "biography" seems insufficiently capacious to describe the singular achievement of Joseph Frank's five-volume study of the life of the great Russian novelist Fyodor Dostoevsky. One critic, writing upon the publication of the final volume, casually tagged the series as the ultimate work on Dostoevsky "in any language, and quite possibly forever."

Frank himself had not originally intended to undertake such a massive work. The endeavor began in the early 1960s as an exploration of Dostoevsky's fiction, but it later became apparent to Frank that a deeper appreciation of the fiction would require a more ambitious engagement with the writer's life, directly caught up as Dostoevsky was with the cultural and political movements of mid- and late-nineteenth-century Russia. Already in his forties, Frank undertook to learn Russian and embarked on what would become a five-volume work comprising more than 2,500 pages. The result is an intellectual history of nineteenth-century Russia, with Dostoevsky's mind as a refracting prism.

The volumes have won numerous prizes, among them the National Book Critics Circle Award for Biography, the Christian Gauss Award of Phi Beta Kappa, the *Los Angeles Times* Book Prize, and the James Russell Lowell Prize of the Modern Language Association.

1976 Perception and Misperception in International Politics

Robert Jervis

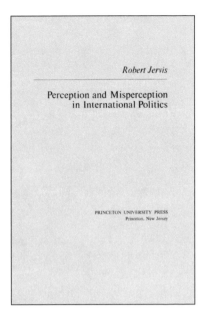

Robert Jervis

Perception and Misperception
in International Politics

PRINCETON UNIVERSITY PRESS
Princeton, New Jersey

This study of percep-
tion and mispercep-
tion in foreign policy was
a landmark in the application of cognitive psychology to political decision
making. The *New York
Times* called it, in an article published nearly ten
years after the book's
appearance, "the seminal
statement of principles underlying political psychology."

The perspective established by Jervis remains an important
counterpoint to structural explanations of international politics,
and from it has developed a large literature on the psychology of
leaders and the problems of decision making under conditions of
incomplete information, stress, and cognitive bias.

Jervis begins by describing the process of perception (for example, how decision makers learn from history) and then explores common forms of misperception (such as overestimating
one's influence). Finally, he tests his ideas through a number of
important events in international relations from nineteenth- and
twentieth-century European history.

In a contemporary application of Jervis's ideas, some argue
that Saddam Hussein invaded Kuwait in 1990 in part because he
misread the signals of American leaders with regard to the inde-
pendence of Kuwait. Also, leaders of the United States and Iraq in
the run-up to the most recent Gulf War might have been operat-
ing under cognitive biases that made them value certain kinds of
information more than others, whether or not the information
was true. Jervis proved that, once a leader believed something,
that perception would influence the way the leader perceived all
other relevant information.

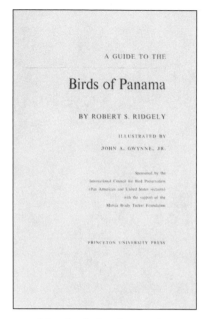

A Guide to the   *1976*
Birds of Panama:
With Costa Rica,
Nicaragua, and
Honduras

Robert S. Ridgely and
John A. Gwynne, Jr.

While serving as an army lieutenant in Panama in 1967, Robert Ridgely was fascinated by the sheer abundance and variety of bird species there, but he was also frustrated by the lack of any reference work with which to identify many of them. When he returned to his studies at Princeton University in 1969, he teamed up with fellow student and fledgling artist John Gwynne to tackle this problem. Over the next few years, during their undergraduate careers, Ridgely and Gwynne created the first comprehensive Neotropical field guide, aided in their research and fieldwork by funding from Robert MacArthur of the biology department and a National Science Foundation summer study program. The result was the first reference book that, with accurate illustrations and informative text, would *really* aid in the identification of birds in much of Central America.

Treating more than a thousand species, the majority of which were illustrated in color, the guide provided invaluable information on every facet of field identification and in turn fueled a burgeoning interest among American and European birders in the avifauna of this region. In 1989, the second English-language edition—and the first Spanish-language edition—further stimulated local and international interest. Today, Panama is in the vanguard of Central American countries committed to ecotourism, owing in no small part to this pioneering book.

1977   *The Passions and the Interests: Political Arguments for Capitalism before Its Triumph*

Albert O. Hirschman

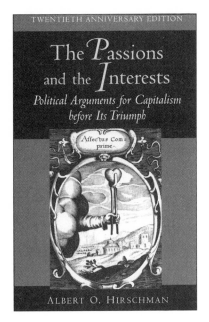

In *The Passions and the Interests*, Albert Hirschman reconstructed the intellectual climate of the seventeenth and eighteenth centuries to puzzle out the intricate ideological transformation that ended up producing capitalism. How was it that the pursuit of material interests, so long condemned as the deadly sin of avarice, came to occupy the role of containing the unruly and destructive passions of humankind? Hirschman offered a new interpretation for the rise of capitalism, one that emphasized the continuities between old and new, in contrast to the assumption of a sharp break that is a common feature of both Marxist and Weberian thinking. Among his startling insights was the ironical finding that capitalism was originally supposed to accomplish exactly what was soon denounced as its worst feature: the repression of the passions in favor of the "harmless," if one-dimensional, interests of commercial life.

In offering his novel interpretation of capitalism's emergence, Hirschman speaks to the full range of scholars for whom capitalism's triumph has become a subject of study unto itself. By injecting human motivation and its unintended consequences into the understanding of capitalism, Hirschman enriches the scholar's appreciation of contemporary economic society.

"Hirschman makes us see the ideological foundations of capitalism in a fresh way," wrote Amartya Sen in his foreword to the twentieth-anniversary edition, despite the "remarkable fact that this freshness is derived from ideas that are more than two-hundred-years old."

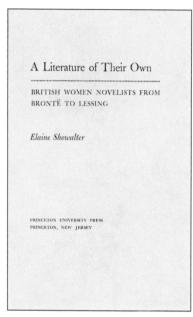

A Literature of   *1977*
Their Own: British
Women Novelists
from Brontë to Lessing

Elaine Showalter

When published in 1977, *A Literature of Their Own* quickly set the stage for the creative burgeoning of feminist literary studies that transformed the field throughout the 1980s and beyond. One of the founders of feminist criticism in the United States, Showalter pioneered a criticism that focused on literary works written by women, which she termed "gynocriticism." Such criticism challenged the traditionally male-dominated literary canon by retrieving and reassessing neglected or forgotten literary works by women.

In *A Literature of Their Own*, Showalter showed how, by examining the plethora of women writers beyond George Eliot and Jane Austen, readers and scholars could discover a lost female literary tradition. This female tradition of literature, she argued, had been rendered invisible by patriarchal definitions of what was important. The book established a canon of works by women that reflected an evolving female consciousness, and it explored the ways in which women writers created "a literature of their own." Launching a major new area for literary investigation, and reshaping the canon of English literature, *A Literature of Their Own* helped to create an explosion of intellectual ferment throughout the humanities that sought to establish "gender" as a category of analysis.

A classic of feminist criticism, the book remains influential today even if the fruits of its revolutionary spadework now enjoy the luxury of being taken for granted.

1979 Philosophy and the Mirror of Nature

Richard Rorty

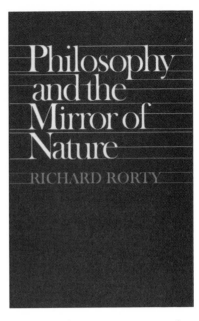

Philosophy and the Mirror of Nature hit the philosophical world like a bombshell. Richard Rorty, a Princeton professor who had contributed to the analytic tradition in philosophy, was now attempting to shrug off all the central problems with which it had long been preoccupied. After publication, the Press was barely able to keep up with demand, and the book has since gone on to become one of its all-time best-sellers in philosophy.

Rorty argued that, beginning in the seventeenth century, philosophers developed an unhealthy obsession with the notion of representation. They compared the mind to a mirror that reflects reality. In their view, knowledge is concerned with the accuracy of these reflections, and the strategy employed to obtain this knowledge—that of inspecting, repairing, and polishing the mirror—belongs to philosophy. Rorty's book was a powerful critique of this imagery and the tradition of thought that it spawned. He argued that the questions about truth posed by Descartes, Kant, Hegel, and modern epistemologists and philosophers of language simply couldn't be answered and were, in any case, irrelevant to serious social and cultural inquiry. This stance provoked a barrage of criticism, but whatever the strengths of Rorty's specific claims, the book had a therapeutic effect on philosophy. It reenergized pragmatism as an intellectual force, steered philosophy back to its roots in the humanities, and helped to make alternatives to analytic philosophy a serious choice for young graduate students. Twenty-five years later, the book remains a must-read for anyone seriously concerned about the nature of philosophical inquiry and what philosophers can and cannot do to help us understand and improve the world.

Negara: The Theatre State in Nineteenth-Century Bali

Clifford Geertz

Combining great learning, interpretative originality, analytical sensitivity, and a charismatic prose style, Clifford Geertz has produced a lasting body of work with influence throughout the humanities and social sciences, and remains the foremost anthropologist in America.

His 1980 book *Negara* analyzed the social organization of Bali before it was colonized by the Dutch in 1906. Here Geertz applied his widely influential method of cultural interpretation to the myths, ceremonies, rituals, and symbols of a precolonial state. He found that the nineteenth-century Balinese state defied easy conceptualization by the familiar models of political theory and the standard Western approaches to understanding politics.

Negara means "country" or "seat of political authority" in Indonesian. In Bali Geertz found *negara* to be a "theatre state," governed by rituals and symbols rather than by force. The Balinese state did not specialize in tyranny, conquest, or effective administration. Instead, it emphasized spectacle. The elaborate ceremonies and productions the state created were "not means to political ends: they were the ends themselves, they were what the state was for. . . . Power served pomp, not pomp power." Geertz argued more forcefully in *Negara* than in any of his other books for the fundamental importance of the culture of politics to a society.

Much of Geertz's previous work—including his world-famous essay on the Balinese cockfight—can be seen as leading up to the full portrait of the "poetics of power" that *Negara* so vividly depicts.

1980 Rome: Profile of
a City, 312–1308

Richard Krautheimer

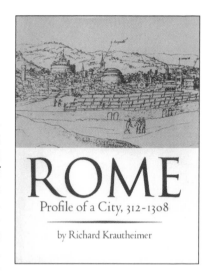

ROME

Profile of a City, 312-1308

by Richard Krautheimer

This magisterial sur-
vey of the art and
architecture of medieval
Rome capped the career of
German-born art historian
Richard Krautheimer. A
renowned scholar of me-
dieval and Renaissance art
and architecture, he had
previously written vol-
umes of specialized art historical research, such as a five-volume
study of Rome's basilica churches with the forbidding title *Basili-
carum Christianarum Romae*. But at the age of eighty-three,
Krautheimer took the opportunity to distill his great learning for
a wider audience. Based on a series of lectures at New York University's Institute of Fine Arts, *Rome: Profile of a City* featured his
erudition but in plainspoken, conversational prose accessible to a
general public.

With 260 illustrations that include photos, maps, and drawings, many of which were made by the author himself, the book
is what Krautheimer called "a thousand-year history of Rome
through her monuments." It comprises two parts: the first traces
the urban development of Rome from 312 to 1308, exploring not
only the often scant physical remains of the city but also the religious, political, social, and economic forces that shaped them.
The second section focuses on reconstituting the evolving map of
the city during the late Middle Ages, from the tenth through the
thirteenth century.

No one can write on the subject of medieval European art and architecture without acknowledging a debt to Richard Krautheimer.

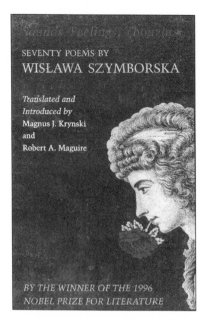

Sounds, Feelings, Thoughts: Seventy Poems by Wisława Szymborska

Translated from the Polish

This book introduced the Polish poet Wisława Szymborska to the English-speaking world fifteen years before she won the Nobel Prize for Literature in 1996. As part of the Lockert Library of Poetry in Translation, the volume typifies Princeton University Press's commitment to publishing poetry in translation by introducing little-known foreign poets to the English language and to an Anglophone readership.

Szymborska was born in Brin in western Poland in 1923. Her first collection of poems was finished in 1948 but was not published until 1952. Several volumes followed as censorship dissipated toward the end of the decade. By the time *Sounds, Feelings, Thoughts* was translated by Magnus J. Krynski and Robert A. Maguire in 1981, she had become a major literary figure carrying on the rich and ancient art of Polish poetry. When bestowing the Nobel, the Swedish Academy commended Szymborska for "poetry that with ironic precision allows the historical and biological context to come to light in fragments of human reality." They also noted the difficulty of translating her poetry, because of its many stylistic variations. Szymborska remains today one of the few women poets to have received the Nobel Prize.

From "The Joy of Writing"

Is there then such a world
over which I rule sole and absolute?

A time I bind with chains of signs?
An existence perpetuated at my command?

The joy of writing.
The power of preserving.
The revenge of a mortal hand.

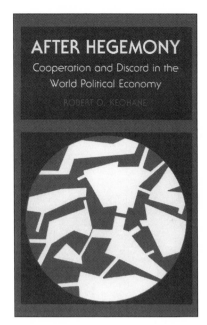

After Hegemony: *1984*
Cooperation and
Discord in the World
Political Economy

Robert O. Keohane

At a time when inter-national cooperation seems threatened by the exercise of American military power in Iraq, it is hard to remember that not so long ago some in the world were concerned about the relative decline of American might. In the early 1980s, postwar institutions such as the International Monetary Fund, the World Bank, and the General Agreement on Tariffs and Trade seemed threatened by the relative decline of the economic and military power of the United States after the Vietnam War and the oil embargoes of the 1970s.

In *After Hegemony* Robert Keohane contended that the continuation of international cooperation and the survival of the great international economic institutions did not depend on the continued dominance of the United States. Rather, cooperation between states had many benefits, and thus states would continue to support the institutions of international economic cooperation and share the burden of their costs as well as their benefits.

Keohane showed how self-interested countries benefited from institutionalized cooperation. The book achieved the rare feat of both providing a powerful answer to a great public debate and significantly advancing theoretical questions in its author's disciplinary field of expertise.

In 1989, in recognition for the importance of the ideas expressed in this book, the author received the prestigious Grawemeyer Award given to acknowledge outstanding proposals for improving world order.

1985   *QED: The Strange*
         Theory of Light
         and Matter

Richard P. Feynman

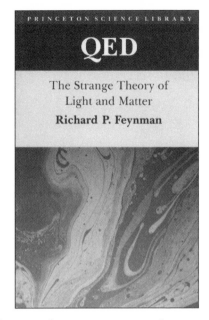

PRINCETON SCIENCE LIBRARY

QED

The Strange Theory of
Light and Matter

Richard P. Feynman

Famous the world over for the creative brilliance of his insights into the physical world, Nobel Prize–winning physicist Richard Feynman also possessed an extraordinary talent for explaining difficult concepts to the nonscientist. *QED*—the edited version of four lectures on quantum electrodynamics that Feynman gave to the general public at UCLA as part of the Alix G. Mautner Memorial Lecture series—is perhaps the best example of his ability to communicate both the substance and the spirit of science to the layperson.

The focus, as the title suggests, is quantum electrodynamics (QED), the part of the quantum theory of fields that describes the interactions of the quanta of the electromagnetic field—light, X rays, gamma rays—with matter and those of charged particles with one another. By extending the formalism developed by Dirac in 1933, which related quantum and classical descriptions of the motion of particles, Feynman revolutionized the quantum mechanical understanding of the nature of particles and waves. And, by incorporating his own readily visualizable formulation of quantum mechanics, Feynman created a diagrammatic version of QED that made calculations much simpler and also provided visual insights into the mechanisms of quantum electrodynamic processes.

In this book, using everyday language, spatial concepts, visualizations, and his renowned "Feynman diagrams" instead of advanced mathematics, Feynman successfully provides a definitive introduction to QED for a lay readership without any distortion of the basic science. Characterized by Feynman's famously original clarity and humor, this popular book on QED has not been equaled since its publication.

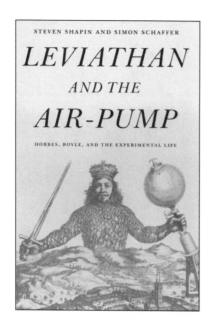

Leviathan and the Air-Pump: Hobbes, Boyle, and the Experimental Life

Steven Shapin and Simon Schaffer

In the aftermath of the English Civil War, as people were groping for new forms of political order, Robert Boyle built an air-pump to do experiments. Does the story of Roundheads and Restoration have something to do with the origins of experimental science? Schaffer and Shapin believed it does.

Focusing on the debates between Boyle and his archcritic Thomas Hobbes over the air-pump, the authors proposed that "solutions to the problem of knowledge are solutions to the problem of social order." Both Boyle and Hobbes were looking for ways of establishing knowledge that did not decay into ad hominem attacks and political division. Boyle proposed the experiment as cure. He argued that facts should be manufactured by machines like the air-pump so that gentlemen could witness the experiments and produce knowledge that everyone agreed on. Hobbes, by contrast, looked for natural law and viewed experiments as the artificial, unreliable products of an exclusive guild.

The new approaches taken in *Leviathan and the Air-Pump* have been enormously influential on historical studies of science. Shapin and Schaffer found a moment of scientific revolution and showed how key scientific givens—facts, interpretations, experiment, truth—were fundamental to a new political order. Shapin and Schaffer were also innovative in their ethnographic approach. Attempting to understand the work habits, rituals, and social structures of a remote, unfamiliar group, they argued that politics were tied up in what scientists did, rather than what they said.

1986 Theology and the Scientific Imagination from the Middle Ages to the Seventeenth Century

Amos Funkenstein

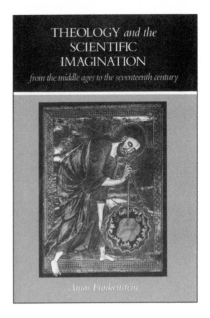

THIS pioneering work in the history of science, which originated in a series of three Gauss Seminars given at Princeton University in 1984, demonstrated how the roots of the scientific revolution lay in medieval scholasticism. A work of intellectual history addressing the metaphysical foundations of modern science, *Theology and the Scientific Imagination* raised and transformed the level of discourse on the relations of Christianity and science.

Amos Funkenstein was one of the world's most distinguished scholars of Jewish history, medieval intellectual history, and the history of science. Called a genius and Renaissance man by his academic colleagues, Funkenstein was legendary for his ability to recite long literary passages verbatim and from memory in Latin, German, French, Hebrew, Yiddish, and Greek decades after he had last read them. A winner of the coveted Israel Prize for History, Funkenstein was born and raised in Palestine and received his Ph.D. in history and philosophy at the Free University of Berlin in 1965, as one of the first Jewish students to receive a doctorate in Germany after World War II.

Author of seven books and more than fifty scholarly articles in four languages, Funkenstein was at the height of his powers in *Theology and the Scientific Imagination*, which ends with the author's influential discernment of the seventeenth century's "unprecedented fusion" of scientific and religious language. It remains a fundamental text to historians and philosophers of science.

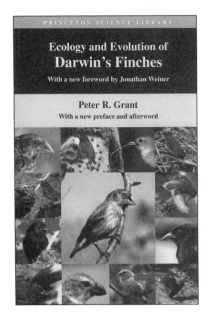

Ecology and Evolution of Darwin's Finches

1986

Peter R. Grant

Variation, adaptation, natural selection, evolution: these ideas developed by Charles Darwin reside so comfortably at the core of evolutionary biology that it is easy to forget the extent to which evolution is a hypothesis. Darwin never saw populations evolving over generations as they adapted to their environment. That, he assumed, would require living for thousands of years. Instead, he saw a lot of traits, including the differently shaped finch beaks in the Galapagos, that would make sense if adaptation and natural selection were at work.

Almost 150 years after *The Origin of Species*, can we see evolution in action? Peter Grant returned to the same finches that Darwin had observed, and, in this remarkable study, he argued that one could observe evolution happening on a scale of months and years, not millennia. By observing how changes in the islands' harsh and fluctuating environment led to natural selection on the size and shape of finches' beaks, Grant showed that competition and selection can act strongly enough on contemporary populations to produce observable and measurable evolutionary change.

Ecology and Evolution of Darwin's Finches is an extraordinary account of evolution in action. Peter and Rosemary Grant have continued to return to the Galapagos and the finches every year. In 1999, they updated this classic book by employing the new tools of molecular biology to determine the birds' ancestry. A few years from now, they will probably return again with another new edition. This remarkable study has produced an evolving book.

1986 A Guide to the Birds of Colombia

Steven L. Hilty and
William L. Brown

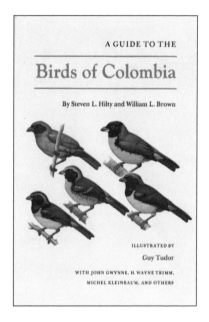

A GUIDE TO THE

Birds of Colombia

By Steven L. Hilty and William L. Brown

ILLUSTRATED BY
Guy Tudor

WITH JOHN GWYNNE, H. WAYNE TRIMM,
MICHEL KLEINBAUM, AND OTHERS

Colombia is perhaps the world's most species-rich country, and yet it has become virtually inaccessible to international birders because of its ongoing civil war. Hilty and Brown's outstanding guide only compounds that irony, tempting readers with its marvelous illustrations and precise and informative text. Robert Ridgely and John Gwynne's *Guide to the Birds of Panama* (see p. 97) had set the standard for Neotropical bird books a decade earlier, but building upon years of field- and museum work, Hilty and Brown's epic contribution managed to raise the bar still further. Indeed it could be argued that in terms of overall quality this guide has yet to be surpassed by any field guide to any region.

A Guide to the Birds of Colombia treats close to 1,700 species, more than half of all the birds found in South America. The sheer number of species, and relative paucity of information for many of them, presented the authors with staggering obstacles. Brown had begun research in Colombia in the 1960s, while Hilty's brilliant field skills were first brought to bear on the Colombian avifauna in 1971. The richly informative text and stunning artwork of wildlife artist and ornithologist Guy Tudor (who later received a MacArthur "genius" award) proved an irresistible combination. Moreover, the book covered many species found in contiguous countries Venezuela, Ecuador, and Brazil, for which there were no guides.

James Binney and
Scott Tremaine

Two of the world's leading astrophysicists, James Binney and Scott Tremaine, here present a comprehensive review of the theory of galactic dynamics at a level suitable for both graduate students and researchers. Their work in this volume describes our present understanding of the structure and dynamics of stellar systems such as galaxies and star clusters.

Nicknamed "the Bible of galactic dynamics," this book has become a classic treatise, well known and widely used by researchers and students of galactic astrophysics and stellar dynamics. Praised for its modern approach, as well as for the rigor and exemplary clarity with which the authors handle the material in this book, *Galactic Dynamics* includes classic results and data while also reflecting the many recent developments in the field. The authors maintain an effective style of exposition throughout, keeping clear what is present knowledge and what is still speculation, while allowing the reader to grasp an overview of the subject before following through (where needed) with the mathematical detail. Most of the astronomical community since the late 1980s was introduced to galactic dynamics through *Galactic Dynamics*, and it remains the most widely used graduate textbook in galactic astrophysics today. No other book gathers together and presents our current understanding of the field in such a clear and concise way. Through this approach, Binney and Tremaine succeeded in creating a classic reference of enormous pedagogic value.

1987– *The Collected Papers*
of Albert Einstein

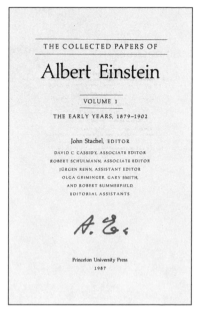

THE COLLECTED PAPERS OF

Albert Einstein

VOLUME 1

THE EARLY YEARS, 1879–1902

John Stachel, EDITOR

DAVID C. CASSIDY, ASSOCIATE EDITOR
ROBERT SCHULMANN, ASSOCIATE EDITOR
JÜRGEN RENN, ASSISTANT EDITOR
OLGA GRIMINGER, GARY SMITH,
AND ROBERT SUMMERFIELD
EDITORIAL ASSISTANTS

Princeton University Press
1987

The Collected Papers of Albert Einstein is one of the most ambitious publishing ventures ever undertaken in the documentation of the history of science. Selected from among more than 40,000 documents contained in the personal collection of Albert Einstein now housed at the Albert Einstein Archives at Hebrew University, and 15,000 Einstein and Einstein-related documents discovered by the editors since the beginning of the Einstein Project, the *Collected Papers* will provide the first complete picture of a massive written legacy that ranges from Einstein's first work on the special and general theories of relativity and the origins of quantum theory, to expressions of his profound concern with civil liberties, education, Zionism, pacifism, and disarmament.

Every document in the *Collected Papers* appears in its original language, while the introduction, headnotes, footnotes, and other scholarly apparatus are in English. Upon release of each volume, Princeton also publishes an English translation of previously untranslated non-English documents. The series, when complete, will contain more than 14,000 documents and will fill at least twenty-five volumes.

Beyond its editorial complexity, the project has presented unmatched challenges to successive Press directors. First, the Press has been responsible for the funding and management of the editorial office since its inception—a unique arrangement for a large papers project. And although a publishing agreement was signed in 1971 with the executors of the Einstein Estate, many troubles—legal, editorial, and otherwise—ensued, and the first volume did not appear until 1987. The project has been through six different editors.

Nonetheless, the endeavor is now well established, with nine volumes published. Currently located at and supported by the California Institute of Technology, the project proceeds, under the directorship of Diana Buchwald, in its grand effort to bring forth this monumental collection.

Albert Einstein: Relativity, War, and Fame

Daniel J. Kevles

In 1922, Princeton University Press published Albert Einstein's *The Meaning of Relativity*, a popularization of his theory that has remained in print to this day, and that more than a half century ago Datus C. Smith, Jr., then the director of the Press, counted as one of its "crown jewels."[1] The book was the first in what has become a sizable number of volumes by and about Einstein that the Press has published, a number that continues to grow as successive editions of his writings appear.

Albert Einstein burst upon the world of physics in 1905, at age twenty-six, when he was working as an examiner in the Swiss patent office in Bern and published three extraordinary scientific papers. One, speaking to the developing though somewhat controversial atomic theory of matter, demonstrated the reality of atoms and molecules. The other two—one advancing a quantum theory of light, the other proposing the special theory of relativity—contributed decisively to the revolution in physics that marked the twentieth century.

Two years later, in 1907, Einstein began work on what became the general theory of relativity. The special theory discarded the assumption of Newtonian physics that there exists an absolute frame of reference in space against which all motion in the universe can be measured. Taking no frame as privileged, it related how phenomena occurring in one inertial frame—that is, one moving at constant velocity—would appear in a second moving in relation to the first. The two frames might be, for example, two trains traveling at different constant speeds on neighboring tracks. The question that started Einstein on what became the general theory of relativity concerned whether the relativity principle could be applied to gravitation. His efforts were greatly aided by an epiphany that inertial mass (that is, mass that resists a change in its motion) and gravitational mass (that is, mass that is attracted by other mass at a distance) are equivalent.[2] That insight led Einstein to examine gravitational phenomena in frames of reference that are not inertial, but that are accelerating with respect to each other.

In 1909 Einstein left the Swiss patent office for a position at the University of Zurich; he moved to professorships in Prague in 1911 and at the Polytechnic in Zurich in 1912. In 1914, he became a professor at the University of Berlin, the director of the Kaiser Wilhelm Institute for Physics, and a member of the Prussian Academy of Sciences. During much of this time, he struggled through writing a series of papers on gravitation, producing what he later described as a "chain of errors." By November 1915, the struggle had brought him to "the final release from misery"—a general theory of relativity that he found excitingly complete. The theory deprived space of its independent three-dimensional existence, holding that it is a four-dimensional manifold defined by time as well as extension and is configured by the mass within it. The theory incorporated Newton's laws as special cases in all frames of reference. It explained a peculiarity in the orbital motion of the planet Mercury that had long puzzled astronomers. And it predicted that the path of starlight would bend and the frequency of atomic spectra would change in the neighborhood of an enormous mass such as the sun. "The theory is of incomparable beauty," he wrote to a friend.[3]

The atomic frequency shift had not been observed, data bearing on it was much disputed, and the failure to detect it offset the success of the general theory in accounting for the motion of Mercury. Great weight thus came to be attached to the theory's prediction of the bending of light rays by the sun, which had been a consequence of Einstein's formulation from its inception.[4] For several years, Einstein had been encouraging astronomers to look for the bending of starlight when it passed by the sun during a total eclipse. Attempts to measure such light deflection in Brazil during an eclipse in 1912 were thwarted by clouds and rain, and an attempt at observation in the Crimea during another eclipse in 1914 was prevented by both weather and the internment of the would-be observer, a German scientist, in Russia as a result of the outbreak of World War I.

The war quickly severed most contacts between German scientists and those in the nations of the Entente, but, worse, it shattered the amity of international science. In October 1914 ninety-three German professors, among them Wilhelm Roentgen, Max Planck, and thirteen other scientists of comparably high repute, issued an *Appeal to the Cultured World*, a manifesto denying that Germany was responsible for the war, protesting the "lies and defamations" leveled against its conduct in the conflict, and claiming that its soldiers had not committed atrocities in Belgium.[5] Lashing back, angry fellows of the Royal Society of London demanded the removal of all Germans and Austrians from the list of foreign members, and the French Academy dropped the signers of the manifesto. In mid-1917, the eminent French mathematician Emile Picard, a former president of the French Academy of Sciences, told an influential member of the National Academy of Sciences in the United States that "personal" relations of any kind would be "impossible" with German scientists even after the war. They had to be ostracized from the structure and activities of international science indefinitely.[6]

Einstein declined to lend his prestige to the German war effort. He was a Swiss citizen, for one thing, but far more important, he was an enemy of nationalism, especially the Prussian variety, and counted himself an internationalist and a pacifist. He refused to sign the *Appeal to the Cultured World*, preferring instead to join a few other scientists and scholars in publishing an *Appeal to Europeans* that declared the attitudes in the manifesto inexcusable and urged that all educated men of all states should ensure "that the conditions of peace did not become the source of future wars."[7]

In England, Arthur Eddington, an astrophysicist, secretary of the Royal Astronomical Society, a Quaker, and an outspoken pacifist, was eager to maintain relations with scientists in enemy countries. Learning about Einstein's general theory from an astrophysicist in neutral Holland, Eddington recognized its high scientific significance. So did the astronomer royal, Frank Dyson, who obtained one thousand pounds to finance two expeditions to test Einstein's prediction during the solar eclipse that would occur on May 29, 1919, and would achieve totality in the tropics. One of the expeditions, headed by Eddington, went to Principe, in the Gulf of Guinea off the west coast of Africa; the other, led by Charles Davidson and A.C.D. Crommelin, journeyed to Sobral, in northwestern Brazil. From Principe, where the totality of the eclipse lasted for 302 seconds, Eddington cabled London: "Through cloud, hopeful."[8]

Einstein learned about and eagerly followed the progress of the English expedition. Although he reportedly declared later that he had had full confidence that the deflection would be found and would match the magnitude his theory predicted—1.74 seconds of arc—he nevertheless waited for news of the expedition's results with keen, somewhat anxious attentiveness.[9] Then, in late September 1919, in a telegram from his Dutch friend and fellow physicist Hendrick A. Lorentz, he learned that the English expedition had detected a deflection of light by the sun of a magnitude that fell within the range predicted by his theory. In late December two young German physicists verified the predicted shift in atomic spectra and also explained the reasons for the previous failures.[10]

Einstein's letters tell much about his scientific, political, and personal lives, and a growing body of them is conveniently accessible in *The Collected Papers of Albert Einstein*, the authoritative volumes of his writings and correspondence that Princeton University Press began publishing in 1987. Volume 9, the latest, bulges with the letters from January 1919 to April 1920 and reveals Einstein with tangible, compelling immediacy during the months in the aftermath of World War I, when the verification of his theory occurred and he suddenly became a world figure.

In the fall of 1919, as word about the eclipse expedition spread among scientists, accolades poured in from physicists on both sides of the recent wartime divide. Then, on November 6, 1919, a galaxy of British physicists and astronomers gathered in the rooms of the Royal Society of London at a joint assembly of that group and the Royal Astronomical Society to hear a formal report on the results of the eclipse expeditions. Many in the gathering were mindful that if the theory proved correct, the laws of Newton, whose portrait looked down on the crowd, would have to give way before those of Einstein. Eddington and Crommelin reported that light from a distant star had indeed been bent when passing by the sun, and that the magnitude of the deflection equaled within experimental error the quantitative prediction of Einstein's theory. The Nobel physicist Joseph John Thomson capped the historic occasion by calling the general theory of relativity "the greatest discovery in connection with gravitation since Newton."[11]

Within days newspapers made Einstein a figure of global prominence, but his sudden fame was energized as much by his location in the political space-time of the world war and its aftermath as by his identification as the twentieth-century Newton. The French physicist Jean Perrin had reported to him from Paris that it was "a great comfort for everyone here . . . to learn . . . that since the beginning of the great ordeal and throughout its entire duration you always knew where to look for justice." English scientists admired him for having not signed the manifesto of the ninety-three German professors, and a number, including Eddington, relished the fact that the theory of a physicist in Germany had been confirmed by English observations, which they counted as an augury for the restoration of international scientific relations.[12] Einstein, on his part, celebrated the fact that "English scientific men should have given their time and labor, and that English institutions should have provided the material means, to test a theory that had been completed and published in the country of their enemies in the midst of war."[13]

Even before becoming world famous, Einstein had been in demand among physicists, finding the lecture hall overflowing with students and colleagues when he spoke. After the world discovered him, he was deluged with inquiries, invitations, and requests. "At night I dream I am burning in hell and the postman is the devil, hurling a fresh bundle of letters at my head because I still haven't answered the old ones," he complained. The German government valued Einstein as a prime cultural asset and agent of international reconciliation, providing hospitality and attention wherever he traveled.[14]

Berlin in 1919 was beset by shortages and inflation, and Einstein was by no means exempt from the rigors of life in the city. In early September the elevator service was cut off in his apartment building at 5 Haberland Strasse, prompting him to write to his mother that "each exit will involve a climbing expedition." He added, "Much shivering lies ahead of us this winter."[15] His mother, who was living in Switzerland, was mortally ill with cancer. Einstein brought her to Berlin, but although the local housing department had granted him an extra room in his building to accommodate her, the building's owner refused to hand over the room. Einstein had to install his mother and her nurse in his study, where she lay suffering "terribly, physically and mentally," he wrote.[16]

For several years Einstein had been estranged from his wife, Mileva, who was living in Switzerland with their two sons, and had been sending them more than half his salary. However, as the mark weakened in value against the Swiss franc, his support for them had eaten an increasing fraction of his salary—in 1917, all of it. The couple's divorce decree, in February 1919, awarded Mileva the interest on the Nobel Prize money that everyone assumed Einstein would win. (He was nominated the next year by a group of Dutch physicists, Lorentz among them, who said of Einstein that "by making progress in the field of gravitation for the first time since Newton, he has placed himself among the first tier of physicists of all time.") Early in June, Einstein married his cousin Elsa, a widow with two daughters. She brought to the marriage a dowry of more than 100,000 marks, but Einstein continued to feel financially strained. "Earning in Germany and spending in Switzerland is an impossible combination," he wrote to a friend.[17]

Einstein was an engaged political observer. Late in the war, in a letter sent from Switzerland to the French writer Romain Rolland, Einstein averred that Germany had adopted a "religion of power," and that he preferred the harshness of defeat to a negotiated peace: Defeat was the only way to check "this delusion of minds" and break the hold on the country of the military, the nobility, and the landed gentry.[18] Now, in the postwar months, he found redeeming features in Germany's misery, confiding to a close friend that "people here appeal to me better in misfortune than in fortune and plenty, just as this landscape is unbearable in the blinding sun." He likened Germany to "someone with a badly upset stomach who hasn't vomited enough yet." Einstein reckoned that it would do "no harm at all" to exclude German scholars from international society for a number of years. On the contrary, the exclusion might instruct Germany to "understand the attitudes of the 'enemy' so that there [would] be no room for the abhorrent idea of revenge, from which, later, new grief could grow."[19]

Always a rationalist, Einstein hoped that inclinations to hatred and revenge might be leached away through a fair and truthful examination of the war's events, especially the Allied allegations of German atrocities. To this end, he joined a small commission formed in Berlin to probe the accusations, its aim to enlighten people who believed they were "tendentious lies." But he counted it "a pity . . . that the action taken regarding the punishment of war crimes is not international. That only fallible *Germans* should be held responsible, even though bad things happened to prisoners on the French side as well, does not allow for complete satisfaction with this act of justice." He told Lorentz that he understood the "bitterness" arising from the "famous Manifesto of the 93," adding, however, that foreign assessments of German scholars were "too harsh," that the signers of the document had been ignorant of the injustices Germany had committed.[20] In any case, he thought the Allies had a lot to answer for, judging them now only a "slightly lesser evil" than Germany because of the harsh peace terms imposed at Versailles.[21]

Einstein remained transcendently internationalist, and his anti-nationalism put him at odds with Zionism as a move to establish a Jewish national state in Palestine, but he strongly sympathized with efforts to establish a Jewish homeland, thinking that the small size of the colony in Palestine would preserve the Jews there "from any power mania."[22] Einstein's self-identity as a Jew was surely bolstered by the anti-Semitism that he had encountered in his earlier career. He had also long been disturbed by the denial of educational opportunity to talented young Jews in Polish and Russian universities.[23] Now, in postwar Berlin, nationalists and anti-Semites attacked both him and his theory of relativity. "Anti-Semitism is strong here and political reaction is violent, at least among the 'intelligentsia,'" he noted in late 1919 to his close friend Paul Ehrenfest, in Leyden, who was also Jewish.[24]

Einstein dismissed anti-Semitism as inevitable, even if ugly, the product of a kind of biologically rooted exclusionism among gentiles. He found it heart-wrenching to see so many Jews, scientists and others, prostrate themselves to be accepted as Germans even though the majority of Germans did not consider them equal members of society. For Einstein, anti-Semitism was not so much to be contested as sidestepped. The answer to it was for Jews— members of a "community of destiny" rather than of a religion, he thought—to behave as tribally as their enemies, organizing and funding their own institutions of learning. Thus he pledged to do "all that is in my power" on behalf of the effort to establish a Hebrew University atop Mount Scopus, in Jerusalem, an institution that would serve not only Jews in Palestine but all his "tribal companions," particularly Jews from Russia and Poland, whose talents would otherwise "go wretchedly to waste." When in February 1921, Chaim Weizmann invited Einstein to join him on a trip to the United States to promote the new university, Einstein accepted, happy to have Weizmann exploit his name, "from whose publicity value a substantial effect is expected among the rich tribal companions in Dollaria."[25]

When Einstein, Weizmann, and his small party of Zionists arrived in the United States in late March 1921, thousands of Jews greeted them at the Battery, and thousands more lined the streets cheering and waving handkerchiefs as they drove up the Lower East Side. Overflow crowds turned out to hear Einstein lecture, in German, on the theory of relativity, and politicos conferred on the modern Newton the keys to the city and the state. The day they arrived in Cleveland, Jewish merchants closed up shop at noon, and what an astonished reporter called "a swirl of fighting, crowding humanity" kept their two-hundred-car motorcade to a slow pace on the way to city hall.[26]

In Boston, where the Einstein-Weizmann party had been met with a brass band in the morning, then feted in the evening with a kosher banquet, Mayor Andrew J. Peters respectfully declared, "Not many of us can follow Prof[essor] Einstein in his discussion of the mathematical properties of space; but all of us can understand his refusal to sign the manifesto of the ninety-three professors." Princeton University, awarding him an honorary degree in May, officially cited his loyalty to moral standards in having "refused to join with others in condoning the invasion of Belgium."[27]

When Einstein and Weizmann addressed a rally of thousands at the Sixty-ninth Regiment Armory in New York, the politico in the White House wired greetings—"their visit must remind people of the great services that the Jewish race have rendered humanity." President Harding had not wanted to meet Einstein, but he changed his mind once he was told that Einstein had not signed the manifesto of the ninety-three professors and that he was a Swiss citizen. In Washington a few days later, Mr. and Mrs. Harding had Professor and Frau Einstein over to the White House along with a delegation from the National Academy of Sciences.[28] Amid the picture taking the president amiably acknowledged that he did not understand the theory of relativity, but like public officials elsewhere, he clearly understood what Einstein meant to the nation's admirers of science, its Jewish voters, and its frame of thinking about the recent world conflict.

Einstein's trip netted the coffers of the Hebrew University far less than Weizmann had expected, but it did lead Einstein to publish one of the most influential books on the theory of relativity. For some time he had wanted to publish a good, accessible introduction to his theory, holding that one did not yet exist. He had published a brief book in German in 1917 under the title *On the Special and the General Theory of Relativity, Generally Comprehensible*. In 1919 it was being translated into English by Robert W. Lawson, a physicist at Sheffield University who had spent the war interned in Vienna, and who was eager to foster a restoration of international scientific relations, but Einstein thought the book might better have been subtitled "generally incomprehensible." (Planck noted that "Einstein believes his books will become more readily intelligible if every now and again he drops in the words, 'Dear Reader.'")[29]

At Lawson's urging, Einstein had prepared an article on relativity for *Nature* that turned out to be too long to publish there but formed the basis for the introduction to his theory that he had wanted to write. He apparently expanded that treatment into the Stafford Little Lectures that he gave at Princeton, delivering the first in the afternoon after the honorary degree ceremony to a jammed lecture hall. Princeton University Press contracted to publish the lectures as *The Meaning of Relativity*. He was late in delivering the manuscript, and the manager of the Press, Paul Tomlinson, was concerned that the delay might diminish sales. He need not have worried.[30]

Daniel J. Kevles earned his B.A. in physics and his Ph.D. in history, both at Princeton, taught for many years at the California Institute of Technology, and since 2001 has been the Stanley Woodward Professor of History at Yale. He has written extensively on the history of modern science and its interaction with society. He is a member of the Executive Committee for The Collected Papers of Albert Einstein, *which is published by Princeton University Press.*

Notes

1. Datus C. Smith, Jr., to Albert Einstein, December 28, 1949, Albert Einstein Papers, California Institute of Technology, Pasadena, California, document 67–803. I am greatly indebted to Diana Kormos Buchwald for advice about Einstein and guidance through his papers.

2. Einstein to Ehrenfest, Berlin, December 4, 1919, in *The Collected Papers of Albert Einstein*, Diana Kormos Buchwald, general editor, vol. 9, *The Berlin Years: Correspondence, January 1919–April 1920* (Princeton: Princeton University Press, 2004), 163. Hereafter, *CPAE* .

3. Albrecht Fölsing, *Albert Einstein: A Biography*, trans. Ewald Osers (New York: Penguin, 1997), 374, 377.

4. Arnold Berliner to Einstein, April 9, 1919, *CPAE*, 9:15.

5. A full text of the manifesto and list of signers is in Georg F. Nicolai, *The Biology of the War* (New York: The Century Co., 1918), xi–xiii.

6. Picard to George Ellery Hale, July 22, 1917, George Ellery Hale Papers, Archives, California Institute of Technology, Pasadena, California, Box 47.

7. Fölsing, *Einstein*, 346, 368.

8. Ibid., 434–436; Matthew Stanley, "'An Expedition to Heal the Wounds of War': The 1919 Eclipse and Eddington as Quaker Adventurer," *Isis* 94 (March 2003): 57–89.

9. "Still no news about the solar eclipse," he wrote to his mother in early September 1919. Einstein to Pauline Einstein, September 5, 1919, *CPAE*, 9:83.

10. Lorentz to Einstein [September 22, 1919]; Einstein to Robert W. Lawson, December 1919, *CPAE*, 9:201, 96.

11. Thomson is quoted in the *New York Times*, November 9, 1919, 6. The meeting is reported in the London *Times*, November 7, 1919.

12. Jean Perrin to Einstein, Paris, August 28, 1919; A. Frederick Lindemann to Einstein, November 23, 1919; with Arnold Berliner to Einstein, November 29, 1919, *CPAE*, 9:78, 147, 157.

13. Fölsing, *Einstein*, 450.

14. University president to Einstein, January 28, 1919; Georg Count von Arco to Einstein, April 12, 1919; Einstein to Ludwig Hopf, February 2, 1920, *CPAE*, 9:2, 17, 252; Fölsing, *Einstein*, 479.

15. Einstein to Max von Laue, March 27, 1920; Einstein to Pauline Einstein, September 5, 1919, *CPAE*, 9:307, 83.

16. Einstein to Konrad Haenisch, minister of education, the arts, and public education, December 6, 1919; Einstein to Heinrich Zangger, January 2, 1920, *CPAE*, 9:167, 208.

17. Divorce Decree, February 14, 1919; Einstein to Berlin-Schoeneberg Office of Taxation, February 10, 1920; Einstein to Heinrich Zangger, December 22, 1919; Lorentz et al. to Comité Nobel pour la physique, January 24, 1920, *CPAE*, 9:4, 189, 597–598.

18. Fölsing, *Einstein*, 414.

19. Einstein to Heinrich Zangger, Berlin, June 1, 1919; Einstein to Aurel Stodola, Berlin, March 31, 1919; Einstein to Lorentz, August 1, 1919, *CPAE*, 9:44, 15, 68.

20. Einstein to Lorentz, April 26, 1919, March 18, 1920, September 21, 1919, August 1, 1919, *CPAE*, 9:22–23, 303, 93, 68.

21. Fölsing, *Einstein*, 425; Einstein to Max and Hedwig Born, January 27, 1920; Einstein to Hedwig Born, August 3, 1919, *CPAE*, 9:241, 80.

22. Fölsing, *Einstein*, 498.

23. Einstein refused an invitation to lecture in Russia in 1914 on grounds that he didn't want to go "to a country where my tribal companions were so brutally persecuted." Ibid., 489.

24. Einstein to Paul Ehrenfest, Berlin, December 4, 1919, *CPAE*, 9:164.

25. Einstein to Max Born, ca. November 9, 1919; Einstein to Paul Ehrenfest, November 8, 1919, *CPAE*, 9:137–138; Fölsing, *Einstein*, 491–493, 495, 497.

26. *Cleveland Plain Dealer*, May 26, 1921, 1, 2.

27. *Boston Evening Globe*, May 17, 1921, 11; Fölsing, *Einstein*, 502–503.

28. Quoted in the *New York Times*, April 13, 1921; Fölsing, *Einstein*, 502.

29. Fölsing, *Einstein*, 378–379. The English translation of Albert Einstein, *Über die spezielle und die allgemeine Relativitätstheorie. (Gemeinverständlich)* (Braunschweig: Vieweg, 1917), was published in the United States by Henry Holt in 1920 with an appendix recounting the observational verification of the general theory of relativity.

30. The publishing contract was dated May 9, 1921, and the manuscript was due the following month. Paul Tomlinson to Albert Einstein, September 30, 1921; Herbert S. Bailey, Jr., to Peter Wait, April 17, 1953. Albert Einstein Papers, California Institute of Technology, documents 67–885 and 67–953.

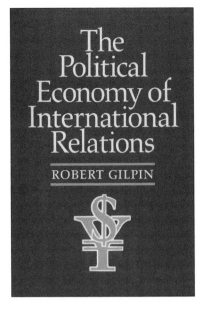

The Political 1987
Economy of Inter-
national Relations

Robert Gilpin

After the end of World War II, the United States, by far the dominant economic and military power at that time, joined with the surviving capitalist democracies to create an unprecedented institutional framework. By the 1980s many contended that these institutions—the General Agreement on Tariffs and Trade (now the World Trade Organization), the World Bank, and the International Monetary Fund—were threatened by growing economic nationalism in the United States, as demonstrated by increased trade protection and growing budget deficits.

In this book, Robert Gilpin argues that American power had been essential for establishing these institutions, and waning American support threatened the basis of postwar cooperation and the great prosperity of the period. For Gilpin, a great power such as the United States is essential to fostering international cooperation. Exploring the relationship between politics and economics first highlighted by Adam Smith, Karl Marx, and other thinkers of the eighteenth and nineteenth centuries, Gilpin demonstrated the close ties between politics and economics in international relations, outlining the key role played by the creative use of power in the support of an institutional framework that created a world economy.

Gilpin's exposition of the influence of politics on the international economy was a model of clarity, making the book the centerpiece of many courses in international political economy. At the beginning of the twenty-first century, when American support for international cooperation is once again in question, Gilpin's warnings about the risks of American unilateralism sound ever clearer.

Richard Wollheim

BOLLINGEN XXXV

In *Painting as an Art*, which began as the 1984 Andrew Mellon Lectures at the National Gallery of Art in Washington, D.C., philosopher Richard Wollheim transcended the boundaries and habits of both philosophy and art history to produce a large, encompassing vision of viewing art. Wollheim had three great passions—philosophy, psychology, art—and his work attempted to unify them into a theory of the experience of art. He believed that unlocking the meaning of a painting involved retrieving, almost reenacting, the creative activity that produced it.

In order to fully appreciate a work of art, Wollheim argued, critics must bring to the understanding of a work of art a much richer conception of human psychology than they have in the past: "Many [critics] . . . make do with a psychology that, if they tried to live their lives by it, would leave them at the end of an ordinary day without lovers, friends, or any insight into how this came about." Many reviewers have remarked on the insightfulness of the book's final chapter, in which Wollheim contended that certain paintings by Titian, Bellini, de Kooning, and others represent the painters' attempts to project fantasies about the human body onto the canvas.

Reviewing the book in the *Los Angeles Times*, Daniel A. Herwitz asserted that Wollheim had "done no less than recover for psychology its obvious and irresistible place in the explanation of what is most profound and subtle about paintings."

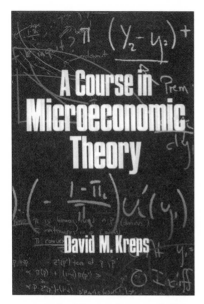

A Course in Micro-   *1990*
economic Theory

David M. Kreps

The late 1980s witnessed the beginning of a revolution in microeconomic theory. Economists incorporated game theory into their standard framework and extended microeconomics into a host of nonstandard topics. Kreps's *Course in Microeconomic Theory* encompassed all of this revolution's excitement and wide-ranging possibilities. Moreover, the book sparked the major revival of Princeton's economics list.

Divided into five parts, the book did not simply cover the well-established ground of traditional microeconomic theory—utility-maximizing actors, profit-maximizing firms, and the price mechanism that joins them—but also applied a more ambitious definition to the entire project of microeconomic theory, arguing that it should encompass "the behavior of individual economic actors and the aggregation of their actions in different institutional frameworks." Such a grand definition meant that the book was less about the solid ground of tradition and more about the blue sky of the horizon. The book showed its newfangled stripes beginning with part 3, "Noncooperative Game Theory," demonstrating how game theory has come to dominate contemporary microeconomic theory. Parts 4 and 5 were equally groundbreaking, addressing questions of information economics and transaction cost economics, respectively.

Kreps concluded his introduction by noting, "All this is, presumably, a bit hard to fathom without a lot of fleshing out. But that's the point of the next eight-hundred-odd pages." That's the point, too, of the past fifteen years: fleshing out the path set by *A Course in Microeconomic Theory*.

1991 *Prehistoric Textiles:*
The Development of
Cloth in the Neolithic
and Bronze Ages with
Special Reference to
the Aegean

E.J.W. Barber

*P*rehistoric Textiles made
an unsurpassed leap
in the social and cultural
understanding of textiles
in humankind's early history. Cloth making was an industry that
consumed more time and effort, and was more culturally significant to prehistoric cultures, than anyone assumed before the
book's publication. The textile industry is in fact older than pottery—and perhaps even older than agriculture and stockbreed-
ing. It probably consumed far more hours of labor per year, in
temperate climates, than did pottery and food production put together. And this work was done primarily by women. Up until the
Industrial Revolution, and into this century in many peasant societies, women spent every available moment spinning, weaving,
and sewing.

The author, Elizabeth Wayland Barber, demonstrates command
of an almost unbelievably disparate array of disciplines—from
historical linguistics to archaeology and paleobiology, from art
history to the practical art of weaving. Her passionate interest in
the subject matter leaps out on every page. Barber, a professor of
linguistics and archaeology, developed expert sewing and weaving skills as a small girl under her mother's tutelage. One could
say she had been born and raised to write this book.

Because modern textiles are almost entirely made by machines,
we have difficulty appreciating how time-consuming and important the premodern textile industry was. This book opens our eyes
to this crucial area of prehistoric human culture.

Men, Women, and   **1992**
Chain Saws: Gender
in the Modern
Horror Film

Carol J. Clover

Are there some aspects of contemporary culture that are too trivial, too low, or just too despicable to deserve scholarly scrutiny? This question was raised by members of Princeton's editorial board when presented with the manuscript of Carol Clover's *Men, Women, and Chain Saws.* Upon reading it, however, they overcame their initial misgivings as it became evident that the shrewdest of critics can find fertile ground in any aspect of our culture.

Clover, a medievalist, had written extensively on the literature and culture of early northern Europe, especially the Old Norse sagas. From her expertise in formulaic narrative grew her interest in contemporary cinema, which is, after all, yet another form of oral storytelling. *Men, Women, and Chain Saws* investigated the appeal of horror cinema, in particular the phenomenal popularity of those "low" genres that feature female heroes and play to male audiences: slasher, occult, and rape-revenge films. Such genres seem to offer sadistic pleasure to their viewers, and not much else. Clover, however, argued the reverse: that these films are designed to align spectators not with the male tormentor, but with the female tormented—with the suffering, pain, and anguish that the "final girl," as Clover calls the victim-hero, endures before rising, finally, to vanquish her oppressor.

The book has found an avid readership from students of film theory to major Hollywood filmmakers, and the figure of the "final girl" has been taken up by a wide range of artists, inspiring not just filmmakers but also musicians and poets.

1993 Principles of Physical Cosmology

P.J.E. Peebles

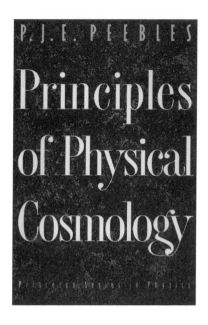

Jim Peebles, Albert Einstein Professor of Science at Princeton University, is the world's principal theoretical cosmologist. His research has served to explain the physics of how the energy and matter that make up the universe evolved from a nearly uniform state just after the Big Bang into the rich patterns, clusters of galaxies, and radiation backgrounds now observed by astronomers. Peebles's theoretical contributions and the powerful statistical methods he developed to test his theories of structure formation ushered in a whole new era in observational and theoretical cosmology, motivating new three-dimensional surveys of up to a million galaxies and inspiring the development of sophisticated computer simulations to compare competing theoretical models.

In this rapidly developing discipline, Peebles's books, particularly *Physical Cosmology* (1971) and *The Large-Scale Structure of the Universe* (1980), have endured as the standards of reference. Then in 1993, Princeton published *Principles of Physical Cosmology*, a successor to Peebles's 1971 volume on the subject. Serving as a comprehensive overview of today's physical cosmology, Peebles's book shows how observation has combined with theoretical elements to establish physical cosmology as a mature science. He also discusses the most significant recent attempts to understand the origin and structure of the universe. The book is, fundamentally, a guide to well-established and notable results, which have stood the test of time, and which form the real foundation for this rapidly moving field's evolution.

Peebles's books abide as classic volumes for students and scientists.

Making Democracy   *1993*
Work: Civic
Traditions in
Modern Italy

Robert Putnam, with
Robert Leonardi and
Rafaella Y. Nanetti

Harvard political sci-
entist Robert Put-
nam is well known for
his contention, first presented in an article entitled "Bowling Alone," that
civic engagement in con-
temporary America is in decline. The intellectual foundation for
his argument was this book, *Making Democracy Work*, based on
research done by Putnam and his associates, not in the United
States but in Italy, contrasting the social and political structures of
the country's northern and southern regions. An examination of
the mechanics of successful democracy, the book has become in
the twelve years since its publication a contemporary classic of
political science.

Putnam argued that northern Italy had flourishing political
institutions because of the complex web of informal and formal
organizations that brought people together, fostered communica-
tions, and increased involvement in the community. He contrasted
this with the comparative paucity of such social organizations in
southern Italy, which had much weaker political institutions.
Economic development did not explain the strength of political
institutions; rather, it was the quality of civic life—voter turnout,
newspaper readership, and membership in associations ranging
from sports clubs to choral societies—that brought about the
strength and efficacy of political institutions.

The book was hailed in the *New York Times Book Review* as a
"rare classic in political science," and in the *Nation* as the modern
successor to Tocqueville's classic *Democracy in America*. The
Economist described it as a "great work of social science, worthy to
rank alongside de Tocqueville, Pareto, and Weber."

1994

The History and Geography of Human Genes

L. Luca Cavalli-Sforza, Paolo Menozzi, and Alberto Piazza

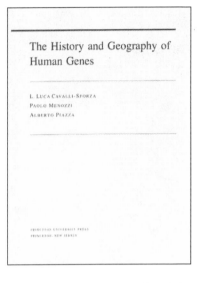

The History and Geography of Human Genes

L. LUCA CAVALLI-SFORZA
PAOLO MENOZZI
ALBERTO PIAZZA

PRINCETON UNIVERSITY PRESS
PRINCETON·NEW JERSEY

L ong before scientists had mapped the human genome, three Italian researchers were at work on another project destined to change the face of scientific inquiry: the reconstruction of where human populations originated and the paths by which they spread throughout the world.

The result was *The History and Geography of Human Genes*, which became not only a landmark in the study of human evolution but a refutation of popular pseudoscientific theory. The book appeared on the shelves at nearly the same time as *The Bell Curve*, the then best-selling book that blamed genetics for the gap between the average IQs of whites and blacks. But Cavalli-Sforza's team concluded unequivocally that once the genes for surface traits such as coloration and stature are discounted, the human "races" are remarkably alike under the skin. There was "no scientific basis" for theories touting the genetic superiority of any one population over another.

The book was far more than a foil for *The Bell Curve*, however. It provided the first map of the worldwide geographic distribution of genes for more than 110 traits in more than 1,800 primarily aboriginal populations. Cavalli-Sforza and his team had become the first researchers to devise a clock by which to date evolutionary history.

The book attracted international media attention for many months in the mid-1990s. The *New York Times* credited its authors with being "able to make sense of the whisperings of human ancestors that are recorded in the genes of present-day people." *Time* magazine hailed the book as "nothing less than the first genetic atlas of the world."

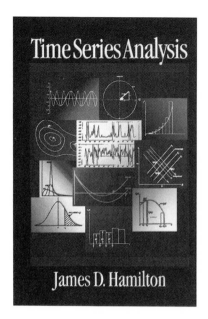

Time Series Analysis

James D. Hamilton

Since its publication just over ten years ago, James Hamilton's *Time Series Analysis* has taken its place in the canon of modern technical economic literature both as a statement of the econometrician's art and as an advanced text and reference work. Econometrics is the mathematical and statistical analysis of economic data. *Time Series Analysis* supplied researchers with treatments of new scholarly developments in econometrics.

As a guide to graduate economics study, Hamilton's book enjoyed popularity among econometricians in seminars in Europe and North America even before it was published. Upon publication, it immediately established itself as required reading for graduate students in economics throughout the world. *Times Series Analysis* has also served steadily as an indispensable work for economists in academe, as well as in government and industry. Jamie Marquez of the Federal Reserve Board in Washington, writing in the *International Journal of Forecasting*, noted: "Hamilton helps translate the new findings into reality for day-to-day forecasting by supplementing them with the new, and technically demanding, background. . . . Anyone interested in modeling macroeconomic developments will profit from opening *Time Series Analysis* again and again."

1994 *Designing Social Inquiry: Scientific Inference in Qualitative Research*

Gary King,
Robert O. Keohane,
and Sidney Verba

The division within the social sciences between those who work with quantitative data and those who work with qualitative data is not simply methodological but reaches to the very idea of what is scientific about the study of society. The divide has sparked battles in nearly all of the social sciences.

Designing Social Inquiry bridged this critical division by arguing that quantitative and qualitative approaches to social science were more alike than different, and by offering a blueprint for social inquiry that could be used by a social scientist employing any method. The authors—all leading political scientists who, in their own research, work with different methods on different subjects—developed a unified approach to description and inference where numerical measurement was not possible.

The book elevated social scientific methodology to a new intellectual level, but it did more than merely contribute to a more rigorous qualitative research design. *Designing Social Inquiry* showed why good research design for quantitative and qualitative research did not significantly differ, and thus why the war between the approaches to social science should come to an end. The book remains controversial and has stimulated a fruitful debate among social scientists. In the words of noted social theorist David Laitin, "The rules elucidated have relevance to statistically minded scholars, formal modelers, comparativists, thick describers, and interpretivists." In short, this book is relevant to every practitioner of social science.

The Nature of
Space and Time

1996

Stephen Hawking
and Roger Penrose

Einstein said that the most incomprehensible thing about the universe is that it is comprehensible. But was he right? Can the quantum theory of fields and Einstein's general theory of relativity, the two most accurate and successful theories in all of physics, be united in a single quantum theory of gravity? In 1994, at the Isaac Newton Institute for Mathematical Sciences at the University of Cambridge, Stephen Hawking and Roger Penrose, two of the most important scientific thinkers of our time, argued over this key conundrum of the twentieth century via six alternating lectures and one final debate. This book captured the liveliness and high-minded quality of their extended argument.

Hawking contends that only a quantum theory of gravity, coupled with the no-boundary hypothesis (the idea that, in the direction of "imaginary time" or before the Big Bang, space-time is finite in extent but has no boundary or edge), can ever hope to explain adequately what little we can observe about our universe. Penrose, playing the realist to Hawking's positivist, thinks that the universe is unbounded and will expand forever. The universe can be understood, he argues, in terms of the geometry of light cones, the compression and distortion of space-time, and by the use of twistor theory (a rather radical new way of describing the geometry of space-time). In the final debate, the reader appreciates how much Hawking and Penrose diverge in their opinions of the ultimate quest to combine quantum mechanics and relativity, and how differently they have attempted to comprehend the incomprehensible.

Mathematics and Science

Robert M. May

Roughly one-third of these one hundred Princeton University Press books (PUP100) fall in the domain of science or mathematics, approximately evenly divided between the two.

Some readers, particularly those who disliked both science and mathematics in school, may ask why distinguish the two. Surely science and mathematics are inseparable, two sides of the same coin. Given that most of this essay will belabor the essential truth of this belief, it seems a good idea to begin by explaining the ways in which mathematics, qua mathematics, does differ from science (as conventionally understood, embracing medicine and engineering).

Mathematics, in its purest forms, deals with logical systems: assume this, prove that. If a triangle has two angles equal, then it will have two sides of equal length. No ifs, buts, or maybes. As amplified somewhat in the brief essay on Gödel's *Consistency of the Continuum Hypothesis*, there can be circumstances when the answer to a well-posed mathematical problem is undecidable, but this theorem itself can be proved.

In contrast, science asks questions about how the world actually works. All answers must be anchored in observations about how things really are. Although it may seem utterly certain that the sun will rise tomorrow, we cannot prove it in the same way as we can prove mathematical theorems within the confines of their closed logical structures.

This being acknowledged, it of course remains true that mathematics and science have been closely entwined since humans first began to inquire about the world around them and the heavens above. We still experience this every day, with 60 seconds in a minute, 60 minutes in an hour, and 360 degrees in a circle preserving the memory of the Babylonians' 60-based number system in practical things, despite its being supplanted by decimal systems in all other contexts.

If we fast-forward to the seventeenth and early eighteenth centuries, we find Newton and Leibniz quarreling about who "invented" calculus.[1] More interesting than this question, I think, is that one of Newton's first applications of this new mathematics was to show that, under an inverse square law of gravitational attraction, spherical planets could be treated as if they were point masses. Increasingly, as the scientific-industrial revolution gathered momentum in the eighteenth and nineteenth centuries, experiment and observation combined with mathematical advances, each stimulating the other, to give insight into essential simplicities underlying much of the physical world. This interplay between mathematical tools, some of them astonishingly beautiful,[2] and scientific understanding is seen clearly in several of the PUP100. Einstein's *The Meaning of Relativity* is an iconic example, but other books by Peebles, Binney and Tremaine, Feynman, Hawking and Penrose, and Anderson speak equally eloquently of the happiness and fecundity of this marriage.

Other books testify to the continuing dialogue between pure mathematics—questions pursued for their own sake, with unabashed motives of curiosity and the pleasure of the chase—and applications to problems of scientific understanding. A notable example is Milnor's book on "Morse theory," with its possible applications, among other things, to quantum field theory.

In short, in the physical sciences mathematical theory and experimental investigation have always marched together. Mathematics has been less intrusive in the life sciences, possibly because they have until recently been largely descriptive, lacking the invariance principles and fundamental natural constants of much of physics. Indeed, it is startling to reflect how recent are the beginnings of the basic task of codifying the diversity of other species which share the planet with us. The canonical date for Linneaus' *De Rerum Naturae* is 1758, a full century after Newton and the founding of the Royal Society in 1660. In many important ways, the legacy of this lag remains with us today.

The longest-serving president of the Royal Society was Joseph Banks, from 1778 to 1820. And what a turbulent forty-two years these were: French Revolution; Napoleonic Wars; much else. Banks, who had briefly studied with Linneaus, sailed with Cook on his first, Royal Society–sponsored, voyage to observe the transit of Venus and onward to the first European mapping of New Zealand and the east coast of Australia. Banks brought back extraordinary collections of botanical and other specimens, eventually adding 13,000 new plant species to the total then known (this, remember, at a time not that long after Linneaus' catalog which in 1758 recorded some 9,000 species of plants and animals in total). However, although Banks, the "flora explorer," may be seen today as one of the pioneers of plant biology, in his day there were bitter quarrels within the Royal Society, where many physical scientists simply did not recognize such atheoretical, descriptive work as lying within the domain of proper science.

Roughly fifty years later we find Darwin, still for me the greatest life scientist ever, writing: "I have deeply regretted that I did not proceed far enough at least to understand something of the great leading principles of mathematics; for men thus endowed seem to have an extra sense." With the benefit of hindsight, we can see how much such an "extra sense" could indeed have contributed to the solution of one of Darwin's major problems. In his day, it was thought that inheritance "blended" the characteristics of mother and father. However, as forcefully pointed out to Darwin by the engineer Fleeming Jenkin and others, with blending inheritance it is virtually impossible to preserve the natural variation within populations that is, on the one hand, observed and, on the other hand, essential to Darwin's theory of how evolution works. Mendel's observations as to the particulate nature of inheritance were contemporary with Darwin, and his published work accessible to Darwin. Fisher and others have suggested that Fleeming Jenkin's fundamental and intractable objections to the *Origin of Species* could have been resolved by Darwin or one of his colleagues, if only they had grasped the mathematical significance of Mendel's results.[3] But half a century elapsed before Hardy and Weinberg (H-W) resolved the difficulties by proving that particulate inheritance preserved variation within populations.[4]

Today, the H-W Law stands as a kind of Newton's First Law (bodies remain in their state of rest or uniform motion in a straight line, except insofar as acted upon by external forces) for evolution: gene frequencies in a population do not alter from generation to generation in the absence of migration, selection, statistical fluctuation, mutation, and the like. Subsequent advances in population genetics, led by Fisher, Haldane, and Wright, helped make the neo-Darwinian revolution in the early twentieth century. In the PUP100, George Williams' *Adaptation and Natural Selection: A Critique of Some Current Evolutionary Thought*, along with work by Bill Hamilton and others, has been influential in further advances and clarifications in evolutionary biology. And, as explained in *The History and Geography of Human Genes* by Cavalli-Sforza, Menozzi, and Piazza, an increasing abundance of data at the molecular level about the genetic composition of, and variability within, populations is combining with computational power to give new insights into how human groups and societies have moved around the world's land masses and over its oceans. Perhaps surprisingly, yet another influential PUP100 book in this context of evolutionary biology is von Neumann and Morgenstern's *Theory of Games and Economic Behavior*. The seminal ideas set out in this work find applications today in many areas of behavioral ecology, particularly in attempts to understand how cooperative behavior evolved, and has been maintained, in groups of humans and other animals.[5]

A paradigmatic account of the uses of mathematics in the natural sciences comes, in deliberately oversimplified fashion, from the classic sequence of Brahe, Kepler, Newton: observed facts, patterns that give coherence to the observations, fundamental laws that explain the patterns. Mathematics enters at every stage in this process of scientific understanding: in designing the experiment; in seeking the patterns; in reaching to understand underlying mechanisms. In biology, of course, every stage in this caricature is usually vastly more complex than in the early days of physics. But the advent of computers, and the extraordinary doubling of their capability roughly every eighteen months for the past several decades, permits exploration—and sometimes understanding—we could not have dreamed of fifty years ago.

Consider the role played by applications of mathematics in sequencing the human and other genomes. This adventure began with the recognition of the doubly helical structure of DNA and its implications, an oft-told tale in which classical mathematical physics played a central role. Brilliant biochemical advances, allowing the three-billion-letter-long human sequence to be cut up into manageable fragments, were a crucial next step. The actual reassembling of the sequence fragments, to obtain a final human genome sequence, drew on both huge computational power and complex software, itself involving new mathematics. The sequence information, however, represents only the Tycho Brahe stage. Current work on various genomes uses pattern-seeking programs to sort out coding sequences corresponding to individual genes, from among the background which is thought to be noncoding. Again, elegant and sometimes novel mathematics is involved in this Keplerian stage of the "work in progress." We are only just beginning, if that, the Newtonian stage of addressing the deeper evolutionary questions posed by these patterns (not least, the surprising finding of the large number of genes we share with other species, and how numbers of genes appear to be uncorrelated with what we regard as the complexity of the organism; rice, for example, appears to have more genes than we do).

In this Newtonian quest, mathematical models will offer a different sort of help from what they provided in the earlier stages, although more akin to the help they give in the physical sciences. Various conjectures about underlying mechanisms can be made explicit in mathematical terms, and the consequences can be explored and tested against the observed patterns. In this general way, we can, in effect, explore possible worlds. Some hard-nosed experimental biologists may deride such exploration of imaginary worlds. And such derision may have some justification when the exploration is in vaguely verbal terms (as it too often still is in some areas of the life sciences). As physicists long ago discovered, the virtue of mathematics in such a context is that it forces clarity and precision upon the conjecture, thus enabling meaningful comparison between the consequences of basic assumptions and the empirical facts. Here mathematics is seen in its quintessence: no more, but no less, than a way of thinking clearly.

The history of the use of mathematical models, and of mathematics more generally, varies among different areas in the life sciences. I referred above to population genetics; ecology and immunology provide two further, and interestingly different, examples.

Ecology is a relatively young subject (the word was coined only a little over a century ago), and much early work was largely descriptive. Seminal studies by Lotka and Volterra explored mathematical metaphors for competition and other interactions among species, but things did not really take off until the 1960s and 1970s, when Hutchinson, MacArthur, Wilson, and others began to ask focused and testable questions in the idiom of theoretical physics. What explains the observed power-law relationship between numbers of species (of birds, plants, butterflies, whatever) on different islands in an archipelago (real islands or virtual islands, as in lakes or mountaintops) and the islands' area? How similar can species be yet persist together? How do the patterns of species' interactions within a food web affect its ability to withstand disturbance? Why are some natural populations relatively steady from year to year, others cyclic, and others widely fluctuating? MacArthur and Wilson's *Island Biogeography*, the initial volume in the influential PUP series of Monographs in Population Biology, focuses mainly on the first of these questions, and did so in a way which marked a seismic shift in the discipline.

At first, some ecological empiricists resented arrivistes, who had paid no dues of years of toil in the field, presuming to mathematicize their problems (sometimes sweeping aside arguably irrelevant, but certainly much loved, details in the process). Others welcomed the newcomers too uncritically. Look, however, at the ecology texts of fifty years ago, and you will find very few equations; today's, by contrast, contain a blend of observation, field and laboratory experiment, and theory expressed in mathematical terms. I think this reflects the maturing state of this vital subject, although it still has more questions than answers. The mathematical traffic, moreover, has not been all one-way: some of the seminal developments in chaos theory were prompted by ecological problems.[6]

Immunology offers a somewhat different picture. Here there are truly remarkable advances in describing and understanding, at the molecular level, how individual viruses and other infectious agents interact with individual immune system cells. And on the basis of such knowledge, so brilliantly detailed on the molecular scale as almost to defy intuitive comprehension, we can, for example, design drugs that suppress viral replication. Chemotherapy against HIV is one notable example. At the same time, however, there is as yet no agreed explanation for why there is so long, and so variable, an interval between infection with HIV and the onset of AIDS. Indeed, I guess that many researchers in this field do not even think about this question, much less recognize that it has not yet been answered. But I suspect the answer may necessarily involve understanding how whole populations of different strains of HIV interact with whole populations of different kinds of immune system cells, within infected individuals. And understanding the nonlinear dynamics of such a system will require mathematical models, with similarities to, and differences from, those that have helped us understand population-level problems in ecology and the epidemiology of infectious diseases.[7] It may even be that the design of effective vaccines against protean agents like HIV or malaria will require such population-level understanding. As yet, this maturation from technically superb description at the level of individual cells and invasive agents (viruses, etc.), to fundamental dynamical understanding at the level of populations of cells and agents, is in its early stages. Today, understanding in the idiom of theoretical physics is even less to be found in immunology textbooks than were mathematical models in ecology texts a generation ago. I venture to predict that the corresponding immunology texts will indeed look different in, say, twenty years' time. In the meanwhile, however, immunology awaits its MacArthur and Wilson.

I must emphasize that none of this is intended to belittle purely descriptive work. It is the foundation on which all subsequent structures rest. For this reason, I was pleased to see two "bird guides"—Ridgely and Gwynne's *Guide to the Birds of Panama: With Costa Rica, Nicaragua, and Honduras* and Hilty and Brown's *Guide to the Birds of Colombia*—among the PUP100. These and their kin are multidimensional: scholarly tools for ever larger cadres of tropical ecologists; catalogs for obsessive bird-watchers; useful companions for the casual tourist. They can also be highly profitable, as the following tale illustrates. On one occasion, about twenty-five years ago, PUP accidentally included a flyer for some of these bird guides with its customary mathematical books flyer sent to the academic mathematical community. The result: one of the bird guides recorded the highest sales ever for such a mathematics-community mailing, beating any mathematics book.

I, like many of my colleagues, was attracted to a life in science for essentially hedonistic reasons. How endlessly fascinating to be able to spend much of one's life engaged in a game with nature, with the rather peculiar rules of the game being to work out what the rules are. So what about the manuals on how to play this game well? In this regard, the year 1945 was an exceptional one for Princeton University Press, with three remarkable and influential books, all included here in the PUP100. I read Hadamard's *The Psychology of Invention in the Mathematical Field* as saying that there simply are no recipes for invention, but that a lot of odd stuff happens in what might best be called "the subconscious." Pólya's *How to Solve It* is simply stunning but, like Hadamard, should never be mistaken for suggesting there is a recipe for, or routine route to, success. If every young teen were to read Pólya's book, and be exposed to the intellectual pleasures it reveals, a lot more people would major in mathematics! And, to complete the trio, Popper's *The Open Society and Its Enemies* is a magnificent and humane achievement in political and social philosophy. It is, incidentally but not irrelevantly, a book that can be read as a caution against dogma, doctrine, and stultifying bureaucracy; it is a sad irony that some of his earlier work on the philosophy of science has, on occasion, been misread by some academic apparatchiks as a rigid blueprint on "how science is to be conducted" (as if it were some form of exercise in painting by numbers). Forty years on saw another PUP100 trio (two in 1985, one in 1986) of fascinating insights into the existential character of the creative process, by Richard Feynman, Steven Shapin and Simon Schaffer, and Amos Funkenstein.

In most OECD countries today there is much talk of the knowledge economy and a pleasing recognition that the fruits of new knowledge play at least as large a part in productivity growth as do the more time-honored labor and capital. Furthermore, there are many recent studies[8] showing that most new knowledge derives from basic research in university settings (particularly in the USA and the UK), infested as they are by the irreverent young. As I mentioned above, these researchers are, by and large, driven by curiosity. On the other hand, their patrons, these days primarily governments on behalf of taxpayers, are understandably driven by economic practicalities. Such a dissonance of motives has inherent tensions, although it has served us well up to now. However, as the world becomes effectively ever smaller and the knowledge economy a more competitive marketplace, there are signs that research funders and administrators are seeking to do "a better job of managing creativity." I think this is worrying. There are good questions to be asked about how best to help originality and creativity flourish. We do not really understand what made Pericles' Athens or Leonardo's Florence or Shakespeare's London the places that they were. The question is indeed rarely asked, much less answered. In short, the notion of managing creativity is not necessarily oxymoronic, but if any such aim is pursued carelessly, the outcome can be truly moronic. Many hapless readers will be able to provide examples from their own institutions.

These are important questions and worries, which I suspect loom larger today than they did a generation ago. Some of the books in the PUP100 on economic ideas, policies, and management are of some relevance, but I think the definitive work on managing creativity and originality in mathematics and science has yet to be produced. Maybe we should all hope it never will be.

Robert M. May is professor of zoology at the University of Oxford and president of the Royal Society. Trained as a theoretical physicist in his native Australia, May was Class of 1877 Professor of Zoology at Princeton University from 1973 until his move to Oxford in 1988. While at Princeton, May edited the Monographs in Population Biology series while his wife, Judith May, was Princeton University Press's acquiring editor in biology. May was awarded a knighthood in 1996 and was made Lord May of Oxford in 2001.

Notes

1. See Carl Djerassi's 2004 play *Calculus* or James Gleick's biography *Isaac Newton* (New York: Pantheon, 2003).

2. A simple, and quite magical, example is the relationship $e^{i\pi} = -1$ which involves the fundamental constants e and π, and the ethereal "square root of minus one," i.

3. See, for example, R. A. Fisher, *The Genetical Theory of Natural Selection* (reprint, New York: Dover, 1958).

4. G. H. Hardy, *Science*, 28, 49 (1908).

5. See, for example, M. A. Nowak et al., "The arithmetics of mutual help," *Scientific American*, 272, 76–81 (1995).

6. For further discussion, see G. Farmelo, ed., *It Must Be Beautiful: Great Equations of Modern Science* (London: Granta Books, 2002), 212–229.

7. M. A. Nowak and R. M. May, *Virus Dynamics: Mathematical Principles of Immunology and Virology* (Oxford: Oxford University Press, 2000).

8. Publicly funded research, predominantly in universities, accounted for 73 percent of all papers (46 percent U.S., 29 percent "foreign") cited in U.S. industrial patents in 1993–1994. Corresponding sectoral figures are 79 percent for patents for drugs and medicines and 76 percent for chemicals, to a low of 49 percent for electrical components. See F. Narin et al., *Research Policy*, 26, 317–327 (1997).

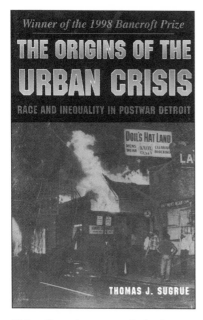

The Origins of the   *1996*
Urban Crisis: Race
and Inequality in
Postwar Detroit

Thomas J. Sugrue

Winner of numerous awards, including the prestigious Bancroft Prize for American history, Thomas Sugrue's *The Origins of the Urban Crisis* offered a bold new way of thinking about the causes of urban poverty in the United States. Using Detroit as a symbol of America's troubled cities and as a lens through which to examine this crisis, Sugrue asked why this and other industrial cities had become sites of persistent racialized poverty. He challenged the conventional wisdom that urban decline was the result of failed social programs and racial fissures of the 1960s. Instead, by weaving together the history of workplaces, unions, civil rights groups, political organizations, and real estate agencies, Sugrue found the roots of urban poverty in a hidden history of racial violence, discrimination, and deindustrialization that reshaped the urban landscape following the Second World War.

The *Detroit Free Press* called this work the "most interesting, informative, and provocative book on modern Detroit," but what made Sugrue's book so important was that its findings were not unique to Detroit. Sugrue argued that the racial tensions, segregation, and economic inequality that plagued Detroit were prevalent in other urban centers as well. The book served not only as a reinterpretation of historical facts but also as a reference point for those looking to improve urban conditions throughout the country. As one reviewer said, "By offering a clearer picture of how the urban crisis began, Sugrue brings us a little bit closer to finding a way to end it."

1997 The Econometrics of Financial Markets

John Y. Campbell,
Andrew W. Lo, and
A. Craig MacKinlay

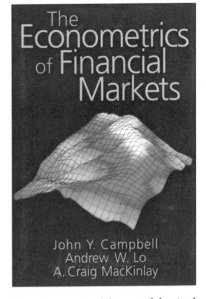

Sometimes you just have to clench your teeth and go for the differential matrix algebra. And the central limit theorems. Together with the maximum likelihood techniques. And the static mean variance portfolio theory. Not forgetting the dynamic asset pricing models. And these are just the tools you need before you can start making empirical inferences in financial economics." So wrote Ruben Lee, playfully, in a review of *The Econometrics of Financial Markets*, winner of TIAA-CREF's 1997 Paul A. Samuelson Award.

In 1952 economist Harry M. Markowitz, who in 1990 won the Nobel Prize in Economics, published his landmark thesis "Portfolio Selection" as an article in the *Journal of Finance*, and financial economics was born. Over the subsequent decades, this young and burgeoning field saw many advances in theory but few in econometric technique or empirical results. Then, nearly four decades later, Campbell, Lo, and MacKinlay's *The Econometrics of Financial Markets* made a bold leap forward by integrating theory and empirical work. The three economists combined their own pathbreaking research with a generation of foundational work in modern financial theory and research. The book includes treatment of topics from the predictability of asset returns to the capital asset pricing model and arbitrage pricing theory, from statistical fractals to chaos theory.

Read widely in academe as well as in the business world, *The Econometrics of Financial Markets* has become a new landmark in financial economics, extending and enhancing the Nobel Prize–winning work established by the early trailblazers in this important field.

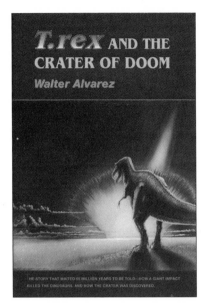

T. rex *and the Crater of Doom*

1997

Walter Alvarez

What killed off the dinosaurs sixty-five million years ago? Until 1980, the question wasn't even seriously pursued. Then Walter Alvarez and several colleagues at the University of California, Berkeley (including his Nobel Prize–winning father, Luis Alvarez), discovered an unusually large layer of iridium in a stratum of rock dating back sixty-five million years. Because iridium is rare on Earth but quite common in meteorites and asteroids, they hypothesized that the only way so much iridium could have been deposited at one point in time was through extraterrestrial means. A massive meteor, asteroid, or even a comet, had to have hit the Earth.

Subsequent work confirmed the discovery of the iridium layer at seventy-five other sites, each at the sixty-five-million-year mark. However, the findings still begged one critical question. If something hit Earth, and it was big enough to kill off the dinosaurs, where is the huge crater it must have left? In 1991, the smoking gun was found: a 180km-wide impact crater on the northern coast of the Yucatán Peninsula in Mexico—discovered by Mexican geologists in 1950, but unknown to scientists elsewhere until 1991—was determined to be sixty-five million years old.

Told by the chief protagonist, Alvarez's book reads like a detective story, as it guides the reader through the events that led to the identification of the crater, and as it provides evidence for the cataclysm that, in just one instant, changed our world forever.

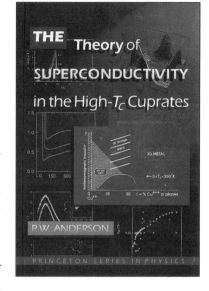

1997   The Theory of Superconductivity in the High-T_c Cuprates

P. W. Anderson

In 1977, Phil Anderson, while working at AT&T Bell Laboratories, won the Nobel Prize in Physics (with Sir Nevill F. Mott and John H. van Vleck) for fundamental theoretical investigations into the electronic structure of magnetic and disordered systems. The applications of this research are extraordinarily wide-ranging, from economics, to biology, to computer science.

Now the Joseph Henry Professor of Physics Emeritus at Princeton University, Anderson is internationally celebrated for his dedicated and insightful theoretical research on high-T_c superconductivity. This book was the long-awaited full presentation of his theory of high-T_c superconductivity in the cuprates. (Cuprates are ceramic materials that superconduct at temperatures much higher than should be possible according to conventional theory.) Superconductivity is a remarkable phenomenon that occurs in certain materials at low temperatures, characterized by the complete absence of electrical resistance and the damping of any interior magnetic flux. Anderson realized that explaining superconductivity required not a new mechanism or "gimmick" but a radical reworking of the electronic theory of metals.

This book contains full discussions of the experimental situation involving these complex materials, and also the latest research done by Anderson and collaborators to advance the development of a theory of high-temperature superconductivity. Since there is as yet no complete theory of high-temperature superconductivity, Anderson's encapsulation of what is currently known and unknown has made this book indispensable to theoretical discussions of superconductivity.

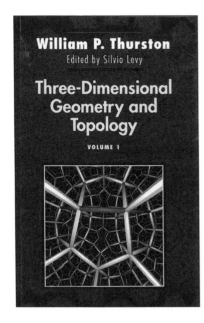

Three-Dimensional Geometry and Topology

William P. Thurston

1997

This book was the origin of a grand scheme developed by Thurston that is now coming to fruition. In the 1920s and 1930s the mathematics of two-dimensional spaces was formalized. It was Thurston's goal to do the same for three-dimensional spaces. To do this, he had to establish the strong connection of geometry to topology—the study of qualitative questions about geometrical structures. The author created a new set of concepts, and the expression "Thurston-type geometry" has become a commonplace.

Three-Dimensional Geometry and Topology had its origins in the form of notes for a graduate course the author taught at Princeton University between 1978 and 1980. Thurston shared his notes, duplicating and sending them to whoever requested them. Eventually, the mailing list grew to more than one thousand names. The book is the culmination of two decades of research and has become the most important and influential text in the field. Its content also provided the methods needed to solve one of mathematics' oldest unsolved problems—the Poincaré Conjecture.

Thurston received the Fields Medal, the mathematical equivalent of the Nobel Prize, in 1982 for the depth and originality of his contributions to mathematics. In 1979 he was awarded the Alan T. Waterman Award, which recognizes an outstanding young researcher in any field of science or engineering supported by the National Science Foundation.

1998   *The Shape of the River: Long-Term Consequences of Considering Race in College and University Admissions*

William G. Bowen and Derek Bok

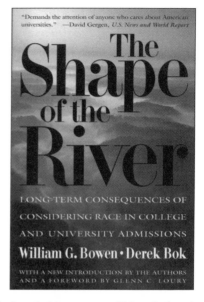

"Demands the attention of anyone who cares about American universities." —David Gergen, *U.S. News and World Report*

The Shape of the River

LONG-TERM CONSEQUENCES OF CONSIDERING RACE IN COLLEGE AND UNIVERSITY ADMISSIONS

William G. Bowen • Derek Bok

WITH A NEW INTRODUCTION BY THE AUTHORS AND A FOREWORD BY GLENN C. LOURY

In *The Shape of the River*, two former university presidents—William Bowen of Princeton and Derek Bok of Harvard—deployed thirty years of historical and demographic analysis to examine the effects of race-sensitive policies in college and university admissions. Their findings supported the case that policies instituted to encourage the broader inclusion of minority students in selective colleges and universities enriched the educational experience of students of all races and backgrounds. Such policies also promoted the successful incorporation of African American and other minority students into the professions, positions of community and civic leadership, and the American middle class.

The *New York Times* wrote of *The Shape of the River*: "Its findings provide a strong rationale for opposing current efforts to demolish race-sensitive policies in colleges across the country. . . . The evidence collected flatly refutes many of the misimpressions of affirmative-action opponents." The book was cited prominently by Justice Sandra Day O'Connor in the 2003 Supreme Court case upholding affirmative action, *Grutter* v. *Bollinger*. Hailed by supporters of race-sensitive admissions policies in colleges and universities, and even by some earlier critics of such policies, *The Shape of the River* went an impressive distance toward resolving the long and heated debates on the role of higher education in dealing with the challenge of race in American society.

Irrational Exuberance   2000

Robert J. Shiller

Robert Shiller's *Irrational Exuberance* predicted that the stock market bubble of the 1990s would burst. Yale economist Shiller argued that the stock market was overpriced, and his prediction came true just as *Irrational Exuberance* was published in March 2000. The book became an instant *New York Times* bestseller and has since been translated into more than a dozen languages. Shiller, now one of the most widely consulted authorities on the behavior of capital markets, advises leaders, writes, and lectures around the globe.

Irrational Exuberance not only predicted the stunning loss of value in the financial markets in 2000; it also provided an accurate analysis of the psychology of overzealous investing, including the aggressive salesmanship of financial professionals and the spin created by a news media that fed what turned out to be the greatest run-up of share prices in memory. The book immediately became a standard work of modern economic criticism.

Irrational Exuberance also paved the way for Shiller's 2003 Princeton book, *The New Financial Order*. In this farsighted follow-up, Shiller presented his ideas for designing financial markets and new forms of insurance to protect people's livelihoods and home values against the depredations of economic misfortune, and to propel forward the economies of developing nations.

2000 *Barrington Atlas*
       of the Greek and
       Roman World

Edited by
Richard J. A. Talbert

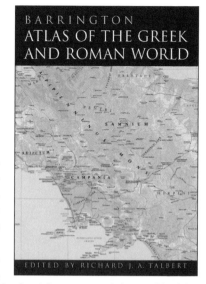

Since the 1870s, all at-
tempts to comprehen-
sively map the classical
world failed—until the appearance of the *Barrington
Atlas* in 2000. With ninety-
nine full-color maps
spread over 175 pages, and
weighing nearly ten pounds, the *Atlas* re-created the world of the
Greeks and Romans from the British Isles to the Indian subconti-
nent and into North Africa, spanning time periods from archaic
Greece ca. 1000 BC to the late Roman Empire ca. AD 640.

The effort to create this monumental work began in 1988 at the
University of North Carolina, Chapel Hill, under the direction of
Richard Talbert, a professor of ancient history. More than $4 mil-
lion was raised to support the decade-long project, including significant support from the Barrington Foundation. Seventy-plus
experts, aided by an equal number of consultants, worked from
satellite-generated aeronautical charts to return the modern landscape to its ancient appearance. They rendered ancient names
and features in accordance with the most up-to-date historical
scholarship and archaeological discoveries.

Classicist Bernard Knox, writing in the *Los Angeles Times*, called
the *Atlas* "an indispensable tool for historians concerned with ancient times . . . [and] also a source of great pleasure for the ama-
teur." Another reviewer praised "the clarity and sheer beauty of
the maps, which . . . make the main volume a sheer joy to handle."

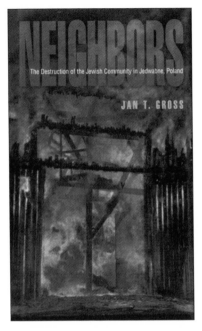

Neighbors: The
Destruction of the
Jewish Community
in Jedwabne, Poland

2001

Jan T. Gross

Even before its publi-
cation in 2001, this
dramatic retelling of
neighbors turned mur-
derers generated unpre-
cedented discussion in
Poland and beyond. Re-
nowned Polish historian
Jan Gross related the
events of one summer day
in 1941 when half of the
Polish town of Jedwabne massacred the other half. Altogether, up
to 1,600 men, women, and children, all but seven of the town's
Jews, were killed—clubbed, drowned, gutted, and burned to death
not by Nazi fanatics but by their Polish schoolmates, grocers, and
friends. For sixty years, this shocking, brutal story had remained
buried.

By stitching together eyewitness accounts with other evidence
into an unusually powerful narrative, Gross compellingly reconstructed the horrific event remembered by locals but overlooked
by his Polish compatriots and unknown to world historiography.
His investigation reads like a detective story, and its unfolding
yields wider truths about Jewish-Polish relations, the Holocaust,
and human responses to occupation and totalitarianism. Gross's
study forced a reconsideration of twentieth-century Polish and
Holocaust history and induced the president of Poland to preside
over a replacement of the previous memorial stone at Jedwabne.

Neighbors provoked so much debate that the Press published
a follow-up volume entitled *The Neighbors Respond* (2004), in
which Holocaust scholars Antony Polonsky and Joanna Michlic
collected articles, interviews, opinion pieces, and transcripts of
public discussions from Poland and elsewhere to shed light on the
intellectual, moral, and historical tensions that arose from the air-
ing of this human catastrophe.

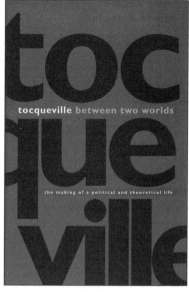

2001 *Tocqueville between Two Worlds: The Making of a Political and Theoretical Life*

Sheldon S. Wolin

Sheldon Wolin is one of the great political philosophers of the past half century, a man who almost single-handedly revived the tradition in 1960 with his *Politics and Vision*. That work, both in its original edition and in its greatly expanded version of 2004 (Princeton), is a powerful critique of attempts to turn political study into a science, and a profound exploration of creative vision in the history of political thought. Four decades later, the publication of this, his second major book, was welcomed as a true event.

Wolin's great achievement is to present Tocqueville in the round, as a man torn between two worlds in several senses—torn between the life of politics and the life of the mind, between France and America, between the old and new regimes in France, and between his own aristocratic past and the world's democratic future. He presents Tocqueville's work as a vital early attempt to grapple with many of the forces that still constrain politics today— the relentless advance of capitalism, science and technology, and state bureaucracy. Though critical of Tocqueville's ambivalence toward democracy, the book was also a paean to Tocqueville as "perhaps the last influential theorist who can be said to have truly cared about political life." As such, it is not only a monument to Tocqueville but a testament as well to Wolin's own lifelong passion for the political.

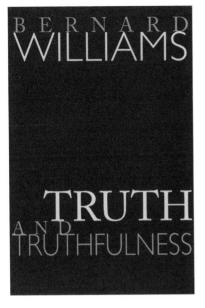

Truth and Truthfulness: An Essay in Genealogy

2002

Bernard Williams

In the late twentieth century, the humanities were wracked by dissent about the status of truth. Relativists, postmodernists, and cynics called into question the very possibility of truth, arguing that power relations alone determine why we give one factual claim priority over another. Traditionalists, especially in analytic philosophy, fiercely resisted this claim. Bernard Williams's *Truth and Truthfulness* had an immediate and therapeutic effect on the debate. Williams sided with the traditionalists in affirming the existence of truth, but argued more importantly that both sides missed a question of much greater significance to human life: What is the value of truth?

Williams's approach to the question, in the tradition of Nietzsche's *Genealogy of Morals*, blends history and philosophy with a fictional account of why a concern for truth might have arisen. Without denying the contingency of much that we take for granted or mistake as true, he defends the virtues of accuracy and sincerity as central to the creation of good individual and social lives. When we lose sight of the value of truth, he wrote, "we shall certainly lose something, and may well lose everything."

The book is a masterpiece of style and substance and a fitting capstone to Williams's extraordinary career as one of the world's most influential moral philosophers. Sadly, he died just a year after its publication, but the book will endure as a landmark in philosophy and a testament to his humanistic achievement.

Acknowledgments

We would like to extend our thanks to the many people who have contributed substantially to making this book happen. We thank Michael Wood, Anthony Grafton, Sylvia Nasar, Daniel Kevles, and Lord Robert May for agreeing to survey our publishing history and write essays. We appreciate the contribution of the numerous advisers who helped us settle on our final list of titles (though of course we take all responsibility for the final selection): Adrian Banner, Alan S. Blinder, Glen W. Bowersock, Robert C. Darnton, Avinash K. Dixit, Caryl Emerson, Peter R. Grant, Robert C. Gunning, Jeffrey I. Herbst, Henry S. Horn, Claudia L. Johnson, Ira Katznelson, Simon Kochin, Stephen Kotkin, Harold W. Kuhn, Simon A. Levin, William Massey, François Morel, Kenneth Prewitt, David Quint, Alan Ryan, Carl E. Schorske, Elias M. Stein, Jeffrey L. Stout, Charles Weibel, Arthur S. Wightman, Sean Wilentz, and Michael Wood. The following former employees of the Press were also essential in reminding us about older titles: Herb Bailey, Joanna Hitchcock, Bill McGuire, Elizabeth Powers, Ed Tenner, and Sandy Thatcher. We thank the Press's editors, who wrote most of the entries on individual books for this volume: Fred Appel, Robert Baggaley, Peter Dougherty, Sam Elworthy, Ingrid Gnerlich, Nancy Grubb, Vickie Kearn, Robert Kirk, Ian Malcolm, Chuck Myers, Anne Savarese, Tim Sullivan, Brigitta van Rheinberg, and Hanne Winarsky. We thank Maria Lindenfeldar for writing the design essay and Eric Rohmann for writing the Bollingen piece. We would also like to thank other Press employees past and present who wrote entries or helped out in other ways on the book: Martha Camp, Pat Carroll, Chuck Creesy, Persa Ducko, Ellen Foos, Adam Fortgang, Gary Frazee, Beth Gianfagna, Alison Kalett, Dimitri Karetnikov, Lauren Lepow, Neil Litt, Annetta Miller, Paul Olchvary, Alycia Somers, Debbie Tegarden, and Nathan Traylor. Finally, we would like to thank Mary Murrell, our former anthropology and literature editor at the Press, for putting this book together. Mary has been indefatigable in her focus on shaping the list of one hundred books, in her pursuit of elusive authors, and in her attention to detail.

Walter Lippincott

Index of Books by Subject

Gillispie, Charles Coulston. 1960. *The Edge of Objectivity: An Essay in the History of Scientific Ideas*, 57

Green, Constance McLaughlin. 1962. *Washington: Village and Capital, 1800–1878*, 60

Gross, Jan T. 2001. *Neighbors: The Destruction of the Jewish Community in Jedwabne, Poland*, 155

Hammond, Bray. 1957. *Banks and Politics in America from the Revolution to the Civil War*, 54

Jameson, Fredric. 1971. *Marxism and Form: Twentieth-Century Dialectical Theories of Literature*, 79

Jameson, J. Franklin. 1926. *The American Revolution Considered as a Social Movement*, 4

Jefferson, Thomas. 1950–. *The Papers of Thomas Jefferson*, 32

Jung, C. G. *See* McGuire, William

Kantorowicz, Ernst H. 1957. *The King's Two Bodies: A Study in Mediaeval Political Theology*, 55

Kaufmann, Walter. 1950. *Nietzsche: Philosopher, Psychologist, Antichrist*, 37

Kennan, George F. 1956. *Soviet-American Relations, 1917–1920*, Volume 1: *Russia Leaves the War*, 52

Kracauer, Siegfried. 1947. *From Caligari to Hitler: A Psychological History of the German Film*, 27

Krautheimer, Richard. 1980. *Rome: Profile of a City, 312–1308*, 102

Lefebvre, Georges. 1947. *The Coming of the French Revolution*, 28

Maier, Charles S. 1975. *Recasting Bourgeois Europe: Stabilization in France, Germany, and Italy in the Decade after World War I*, 93

McGuire, William, editor. 1974. *The Freud/Jung Letters: The Correspondence between Sigmund Freud and C. G. Jung*, 84

Ortega y Gasset, José. 1948. *The Dehumanization of Art, and Notes on the Novel*, 29

Palmer, R. R. 1941. *Twelve Who Ruled: The Committee of Public Safety during the Terror*, 9

Panofsky, Erwin. 1943. *The Life and Art of Albrecht Dürer*, 12

SOCIAL SCIENCE

A Note about Production

This book was designed by Maria Lindenfeldar.

The text typeface is Minion,
designed by Robert Slimbach,
and first issued in digital form by Adobe Systems Inc. in 1990.
Based on Old Style typefaces of the late Renaissance, the
full Minion Pro family contains three weights and two widths,
each with optical size variations.

We would like to thank
NK Graphics, our compositor,
Maple Press, our printer and binder, and
Lehigh Press, our jacket printer,
for generously providing their services at cost for this special project.